Questions and Answers

Questions and Answers

POPE BENEDICT XVI

Our Sunday Visitor Publishing Division
Our Sunday Visitor, Inc.
Huntington, Indiana 46750

Our Sunday Visitor Publishing Division
Our Sunday Visitor, Inc.
200 Noll Plaza
Huntington, IN 46750

ISBN 978-1-59276-439-6 (Inventory No. T676)
LCCN: 2007942823

Cover design by Tyler Ottinger
Interior design by Sherri L. Hoffman
Cover photo by Stefano Spaziani

PRINTED IN THE UNITED STATES OF AMERICA

Contents

Editor's Note

SHORTLY AFTER BEING ELECTED pope in 2005, Pope Benedict XVI found a unique way to encounter various groups in the Church, not only by prayer and a papal address to them, but also a dialogue — in the form of question and answer sessions with the group. This book is a collection of those sessions held from 2005 to 2007 with such divergent groups as young children who had recently made their First Communion, youth, and priests. The questions cover a wide range of topics, as a perusal of the Topical Index in Appendix II will evidence.

In presenting these questions in book form, we have tried to make them as uniform as possible; but, as you will see, this is not always possible. We have added translations of some Latin words (thanks go to Fr. John Zuhlsdorf for completing this task) that were not originally translated when the Holy Father presented the answers. We have also added continuous numbering of all the questions for easy use with the Scripture References and Topical Index provided in the appendices.

MICHAEL DUBRUIEL
Our Sunday Visitor
February 2008

I. Questions Asked by Children

The following questions were asked by children who had made their First Holy Communion during the previous year at an encounter with Pope Benedict XVI at St. Peter's on October 15, 2005.

1. Dear Pope, what are your memories of your First Communion day?[1]

I WOULD FIRST LIKE to say thank you for this celebration of faith that you are offering to me, for your presence, and for your joy. I greet you and thank you for the hug I have received from some of you, a hug that, of course, symbolically stands for you all.

I remember my First Communion day very well. It was a lovely Sunday in March 1936, sixty-nine years ago. It was a sunny day, the church looked very beautiful, there was music. . . . There were so many beautiful things that I remember. There were about 30 of us, boys and girls from my little village of no more than 500 inhabitants.

But at the heart of my joyful and beautiful memories is this one: I understood that Jesus had entered my heart, he had actually visited me. And with Jesus, God himself was with me. And I realized that this is a gift of love that is truly worth more than all the other things that life can give.

So on that day I was really filled with great joy, because Jesus came to me and I realized that a new stage in my life was beginning — I was nine years old — and that it was henceforth important to stay faithful to that encounter, to that communion. I promised the Lord as best I could: "I always want to stay with you," and I prayed to him, "but above all, stay with me." So I went on living my life like that; thanks be to God, the Lord has always taken me by the hand and guided me, even in difficult situations.

---

[1] Question asked by Andrea.

Thus, that day of my First Communion was the beginning of a journey made together. I hope that for all of you too, the First Communion you have received in this Year of the Eucharist will be the beginning of a lifelong friendship with Jesus, the beginning of a journey together, because in walking with Jesus, we do well and life becomes good.

~

2. Holy Father, before the day of my First Communion I went to confession. I have also been to confession on other occasions. I wanted to ask you: Do I have to go to confession every time I receive Communion, even when I have committed the same sins? Because I realize that they are always the same.[2]

I WILL TELL YOU two things. The first, of course, is that you do not always have to go to confession before you receive Communion unless you have committed such serious sins that they need to be confessed. Therefore, it is not necessary to make one's confession before every Eucharistic Communion. This is the first point. It is only necessary when you have committed a really serious sin, when you have deeply offended Jesus, so that your friendship is destroyed and you have to start again. Only in that case, when you are in a state of "mortal" sin, in other words, grave (sin), is it necessary to go to confession before Communion. This is my first point.

My second point: Even if, as I said, it is not necessary to go to confession before each Communion, it is very helpful to confess with a certain regularity. It is true: Our sins are always the

---

[2] Question asked by Livia.

same, but we clean our homes, our rooms, at least once a week, even if the dirt is always the same; in order to live in cleanliness, in order to start again. Otherwise, the dirt might not be seen, but it builds up. Something similar can be said about the soul, for me myself: If I never go to confession, my soul is neglected and, in the end, I am always pleased with myself and no longer understand that I must always work hard to improve, that I must make progress. And this cleansing of the soul that Jesus gives us in the Sacrament of Confession helps us to make our consciences more alert, more open, and hence, it also helps us to mature spiritually and as human persons.

Therefore, two things: Confession is only necessary in the case of a serious sin, but it is very helpful to confess regularly in order to foster the cleanliness and beauty of the soul and to mature day by day in life.

~~~

3. In preparing me for my First Communion day, my catechist told me that Jesus is present in the Eucharist. But how? I can't see him![3]

No, WE CANNOT SEE HIM, but there are many things that we do not see but they exist and are essential. For example: We do not see our reason, yet we have reason. We do not see our intelligence, and we have it. In a word: We do not see our soul, and yet it exists and we see its effects, because we can speak, think, and make decisions, etc. Nor do we see an electric current, for example, yet we see that it exists; we see this microphone, that it is working, and we see lights. Therefore, we do not see the

---

[3] Question asked by Andrea.

very deepest things, those that really sustain life and the world, but we can see and feel their effects. This is also true for electricity; we do not see the electric current, but we see the light.

So it is with the Risen Lord: We do not see him with our eyes, but we see that wherever Jesus is, people change, they improve. A greater capacity for peace, for reconciliation, etc., is created. Therefore, we do not see the Lord himself, but we see the effects of the Lord: So we can understand that Jesus is present. And as I said, it is precisely the invisible things that are the most profound, the most important. So let us go to meet this invisible but powerful Lord who helps us to live well.

4. Your Holiness, everyone tells us that it is important to go to Mass on Sunday. We would gladly go to it, but often our parents do not take us because on Sundays they sleep. The parents of a friend of mine work in a shop, and we often go to the country to visit our grandparents. Could you say something to them, to make them understand that it is important to go to Mass together on Sundays?[4]

I WOULD THINK SO, of course, with great love and great respect for your parents, because they certainly have a lot to do. However, with a daughter's respect and love, you could say to them: "Dear Mommy, dear Daddy, it is so important for us all, even for you, to meet Jesus. This encounter enriches us. It is an important element in our lives. Let's find a little time together, we can find an opportunity. Perhaps there is also a possibility where Grandmom lives."

---

[4] Question asked by Giulia.

In brief, I would say, with great love and respect for your parents, I would tell them: "Please understand that this is not only important for me, it is not only catechists who say it, it is important for us all. And it will be the light of Sunday for all our family."

⌁

5. What good does it do for our everyday life to go to Holy Mass and receive Communion?[5]

IT CENTERS LIFE. We live amid so many things. And the people who do not go to church, do not know that it is precisely Jesus they lack. But they feel that something is missing in their lives. If God is absent from my life, if Jesus is absent from my life, a guide, an essential friend is missing, even an important joy for life, the strength to grow as a man, to overcome my vices and mature as a human being.

Therefore, we cannot immediately see the effects of being with Jesus and of going to Communion. But with the passing of the weeks and years, we feel more and more keenly the absence of God, the absence of Jesus. It is a fundamental and destructive incompleteness. I could easily speak of countries where atheism has prevailed for years: How souls are destroyed, but also the earth. In this way we can see that it is important, and I would say fundamental, to be nourished by Jesus in Communion. It is he who gives us enlightenment, offers us guidance for our lives, a guidance that we need.

---

[5] Question asked by Alessandro.

6. Dear Pope, can you explain to us what Jesus meant when he said to the people who were following him: "I am the bread of life?"[6]

FIRST OF ALL, perhaps we should explain clearly what bread is. Today, we have a refined cuisine, rich in very different foods, but in simpler situations bread is the basic source of nourishment; and when Jesus called himself the bread of life, the bread is, shall we say, the initial, an abbreviation that stands for all nourishment. And as we need to nourish our bodies in order to live, so we also need to nourish our spirits, our souls, and our wills. As human persons, we do not only have bodies but also souls; we are thinking beings with minds and wills. We must also nourish our spirits and our souls, so that they can develop and truly attain their fulfillment.

And therefore, if Jesus says: "I am the bread of life," it means that Jesus himself is the nourishment we need for our soul, for our inner self, because the soul also needs food. And technical things do not suffice, although they are so important. We really need God's friendship, which helps us to make the right decisions. We need to mature as human beings. In other words: Jesus nourishes us so that we can truly become mature people and our lives become good.

---

[6] Question asked by Anna.

⌒

7. Holy Father, what is Eucharistic Adoration? How is it done? Can you explain it to us? Thank you.[7]

WE WILL SEE STRAIGHTAWAY what adoration is and how it is done, because everything has been properly prepared for it: We will say prayers, we will sing, kneel, and in this way we will be in Jesus' presence.

But of course, your question requires a deeper answer: Not only how you do adoration but what adoration is. I would say: Adoration is recognizing that Jesus is my Lord, that Jesus shows me the way to take, and that I will live well only if I know the road that Jesus points out and follow the path he shows me.

Therefore, adoration means saying: "Jesus, I am yours. I will follow you in my life; I never want to lose this friendship, this communion with you." I could also say that adoration is essentially an embrace with Jesus in which I say to him: "I am yours, and I ask you, please stay with me always."

⌒

Concluding Remarks by the Holy Father

Dear boys and girls, brothers and sisters, at the end of this very beautiful meeting I can find one word only: Thank you.

Thank you for this feast of faith.

Thank you for this meeting with each other and with Jesus.

---

[7] Question asked by Adriano.

And thank you, it goes without saying, to all those who made this celebration possible: To the catechists, the priests, the Sisters; to you all.

I repeat at the end the words of the beginning of every liturgy and I say to you: "Peace be with you"; that is, may the Lord be with you, may joy be with you, and thus, may life be good.

Have a good Sunday, good night, and goodbye all together with the Lord. Thank you very much!

II. Questions Asked by Priests of the Diocese of Rome

The following questions were asked by priests of the Diocese of Rome during an encounter with Pope Benedict XVI at St. Peter's on March 2, 2006.

Opening Address of the Holy Father

I WOULD FIRST LIKE to express my joy at being here with you, dear priests of Rome. It is a true joy to see so many good pastors at the service of the "Good Shepherd" here, in the first See of Christianity, in the Church which "presides in charity" and must be a model for other local churches. Thank you for your service!

We have the shining example of Fr. Andrea,[8] who shows us what it means to "be" a priest to the very end: dying for Christ during a moment of prayer, thereby witnessing on the one hand to the interiority of his own life with Christ, and on the other, to his own witness for people at a truly "panpherical" point in the world, surrounded by hatred and the fanaticism of others. It is a witness that inspires everyone to follow Christ, to give one's life for others and thus to find Life.

8. Holy Father, we are meeting you at this Lenten gathering for the first time. I want to remember the beloved Servant of God John Paul II. In the words you spoke at his funeral I saw a sign of continuity between you and your beloved predecessor: "We can be sure that our beloved Pope is standing today at the window of the Father's House, that he sees us and blesses us." This thought

---

[8] Fr. Andrea Santoro, an Italian priest, was murdered in Santa Maria Church in Trabzon, Turkey, on February 5, 2006.

inspires a sonnet written in Roman dialect that I have dedicated to you: "A window on high in Heaven."

WITH REGARD TO THE FIRST QUESTION, I first of all say a big "thank you" for this marvelous poem! There are also poets and artists in the Church of Rome, in the presbyterate of Rome, and I will have the possibility of further meditating upon and interiorizing these beautiful words, mindful that this "window" is always "open." Perhaps this is an opportunity to recall the fundamental legacy of the great Pope John Paul II in order to continue to increasingly assimilate this legacy.

Yesterday, we began Lent. Today's liturgy gives us a profound idea of the essential significance of Lent: It is a guide for our life. It therefore seems to me — I speak with reference to Pope John Paul II — that we should insist a little on today's First Reading. Moses' great discourse, on the threshold of the Holy Land after the 40-year pilgrimage in the desert, sums up the whole of the Torah, the whole of the Law. Here we find the essential, not only for the Jewish people but also for us. This essential is the Word of God: "I have set before you life and death, blessing and curse; therefore choose life" (Dt. 30:19).

These fundamental words of Lent are also the fundamental words of the legacy of our great Pope John Paul II: "Choose life." This is our priestly vocation: To choose life ourselves and to help others to choose life. It is a matter of renewing in Lent our own, so to speak, "fundamental option" — the option for life.

But the question immediately arises: How can we choose life, how should we do this? Reflecting upon this, I remembered that the great defection from Christianity that has occurred in the West in the past 100 years was precisely in the name of the option for life. It was said — I am thinking of Nietzsche but also of so many others — that Christianity is an option opposed to life. With the Cross, with all the Commandments, with all the "no's" that it proposes to us, some have said that it closes the door to life.

But we, we want to have life, and we choose, we opt, ultimately, for life, freeing ourselves by the Cross, freeing ourselves by all these Commandments, by all these "no's." We want to have life in abundance, nothing but life.

Here, the words of today's Gospel immediately come to mind: "Whoever would save his life will lose it; and whoever loses his life for my sake, he will save it" (Lk. 9:24). This is the paradox we must first be aware of in opting for life. It is not by asserting one's right to life but only by giving life, not by having life and holding on to it but by giving it, that we can find it. This is the ultimate meaning of the Cross: Not to seek life for oneself, but to give one's own life.

Thus, the New and Old Testaments go together. In the First Reading from Deuteronomy God's response is: "I command you this day, by loving the Lord your God, by walking in his ways, and by keeping his commandments and his statutes and his ordinances, then you shall live" (Dt. 30:16). At first sight we may not like this, but it is the way: The option for life and the option for God are identical. The Lord says so in St. John's Gospel: "This is eternal life, that they know you" (Jn. 17:3).

Human life is a relationship. It is only in a relationship, and not closed in on ourselves, that we can have life. And the fundamental relationship is the relationship with the Creator, or else other relations are fragile. Hence, it is essential to choose

God. A world empty of God, a world that has forgotten God, loses life and relapses into a culture of death.

Choosing life, taking the option for life, therefore, means first and foremost choosing the option of a relationship with God. However, the question immediately arises: With which God? Here, once again, the Gospel helps us: With the God who showed us his face in Christ, the God who overcame hatred on the Cross, that is, in love to the very end. Thus, by choosing this God, we choose life.

Pope John Paul II gave us the great Encyclical *Evangelium Vitae.* In it we can clearly see — it is, as it were, a portrait of the problems of today's culture, hopes and dangers — that a society that forgets God, excludes God, precisely in order to have life, falls into a culture of death.

Precisely in order to have life, a "no" is said to the child, because it takes some part of my life away from me; a "no" is said to the future, in order to have the whole of the present; a "no" is said to unborn life as well as to suffering life that is approaching death. What seems to be a culture of life becomes the anticulture of death, where God is absent, where that God who does not ordain hatred but overcomes hatred is absent. Here we truly opt for life.

Consequently, everything is connected: The deepest option for the Crucified Christ with the most complete option for life, from the very first moment until the very last.

To me this also seems in some way the nucleus of our pastoral care: to help people make the true choice for life, to renew their relationship with God as the relationship that gives us life and shows us the way to life. And thus, to love Christ anew, who from being the most unknown Being whom we did not reach and who remained enigmatic, became a known God, a God with a human face, a God who is love.

Let us keep this fundamental point for life before us and consider that this program contains the whole Gospel, the Old and the New Testaments, that center on Christ. Lent should be for us a time to renew our knowledge of God, our friendship with Jesus, to be able to guide others in a convincing way to opt for life, which is above all the option for God. It must be clear to us that in choosing Christ, we have not chosen to deny life, but have really chosen life in abundance.

The Christian option is basically very simple: It is the option to say "yes" to life. But this "yes" only takes place with a God who is known, with a God with a human face. It takes place by following this God in the communion of love. What I have said so far is intended as a way of renewing our remembrance of the great Pope John Paul II.

9. As a parish priest, I ask you for a few words of joyful encouragement for mothers. In memory of our mothers, Your Holiness, for their faith and spiritual strength that can be seen in the human and Christian upbringing that they gave to us, help us talk to the mothers of all the boys and girls who attend catechism classes and are often distracted. Say a few words that we can pass on to them, saying: "This is what the Pope says to you."

WE COME TO THE SECOND question, which was so nice, about mothers. I would say that I cannot communicate important programs just now, words that you could say to mothers. Simply tell them: The Pope thanks you! He thanks you because you have given life, because you want to help this life that is developing and thereby to build a human world, contributing to a human future.

And it is not only by giving biological life that you do so, but by communicating the heart of life, making Jesus known, introducing your children to knowledge of Jesus and friendship with Jesus. This is the foundation of every catechesis.

Therefore, one must thank mothers above all because they have had the courage to give life. And we must ask mothers to complete their gift by giving friendship with Jesus.

10. The Blessed Sacrament is exposed for adoration 24 hours a day in St. Anastasia on the Palatine. The faithful take turns in making Perpetual Adoration. My suggestion is that there should be Perpetual Adoration of the Eucharist in each one of the five sectors of the Diocese of Rome.

THE THIRD QUESTION was by the Rector of St. Anastasia's Church. Here, perhaps I can say in parentheses that the Church of St. Anastasia was already dear to me even before I saw it because it was the titular church of our Cardinal de Faulhaber. He would always let us know that he had a church in Rome, St. Anastasia's. We always met with this community for the second Mass of Christmas, dedicated to the *"statio"*[9] of St. Anastasia.

---

[9] Latin for "station," as in the ancient Roman custom of "station churches" during all of Lent, Sundays of Advent, Ember Days, and other great feasts. There were 84 station days. This is a custom that goes back to at least of the time of St. Gregory the Great (d. 604). The people would gather at one church for initial prayers, the "collect" church, and then process to another Church, the "stopping point" or "station" church for Mass. The custom is maintained in Rome even today, especially by the

Historians say that it was at St. Anastasia's that the Pope had to visit the Byzantine governor and that it was there that he had his seat. The church also reminds us of the saint, and hence, of the "Anastasis."[10] At Christmas we also think of the Resurrection.

I did not know and I am glad to have been told about it, that the church is now a place of "Perpetual Adoration"; thus, it is a focal point in Rome of the life of faith. I confidently place in the hands of the Cardinal Vicar this proposal to create five places of Perpetual Adoration in the five sectors of the Diocese of Rome.

I only want to say: Thanks be to God that after the Council, after a period in which the sense of Eucharistic Adoration was somewhat lacking, the joy of this adoration was reborn everywhere in the Church, as we saw and heard at the Synod on the Eucharist. Of course, the conciliar Constitution on the Liturgy enabled us to discover to the full the riches of the Eucharist in which the Lord's testament is accomplished: He gives himself to us, and we respond by giving ourselves to him. We have now rediscovered, however, that without adoration as an act consequent to Communion received, this center that the Lord gave to us, that is, the possibility of celebrating his sacrifice and thus of entering into a sacramental, almost corporeal, communion with him, loses its depth as well as its human richness.

Adoration means entering the depths of our hearts in communion with the Lord, who makes himself bodily pres-

---

seminarians of the North American College and by a Roman confraternity dedicated to the martyrs and saints of Rome. Even today the 2002 *Roman Missal* recommends this practice for dioceses.

[10] Greek for "resurrection." There is a word play between the name of the "station" church for second of the three traditional Christmas Masses, St. Anastasia, and the Greek word for "resurrection." The Basilica of St. Anastasia, next to the Circus Maximus, was one of the original 25 *tituli* or roughly "parish churches" of ancient Rome. St. Anastasia's name was added to the Roman Canon in the fifth century.

ent in the Eucharist. In the monstrance, he always entrusts himself to us and asks us to be united with his Presence, with his risen Body.

⌒

11. You are a "teacher" who guides thought in a "fully human" faith. We never fail to be moved by your words, by the harmony in which each point finds its mark, in lively synthesis, especially in a time as fragmented as ours. How can we help lay people grasp this synthesis of harmony, this catholicity of faith?

WE NOW COME to the fourth question. If I have understood it correctly, but I am not sure if I have, it was: "How do we acquire a living faith, a truly Catholic faith, a faith that is practical, lively, and effective?"

Faith, ultimately, is a gift. Consequently, the first condition is to let ourselves be given something, not to be self-sufficient or do everything by ourselves — because we cannot — but to open ourselves in the awareness that the Lord truly gives.

It seems to me that this gesture of openness is also the first gesture of prayer: being open to the Lord's presence and to his gift. This is also the first step in receiving something that we do not have, that we cannot have with the intention of acquiring it all on our own.

We must make this gesture of openness, of prayer — give me faith, Lord! — with our whole being. We must enter into this willingness to accept the gift and let ourselves, our thoughts, our affections, and our will, be completely immersed in this gift.

Here, I think it is very important to stress one essential point: No one believes purely on his own. We always believe in and with the Church. The Creed is always a shared act, it means letting ourselves be incorporated into a communion of progress, life, words, and thought.

We do not "have" faith, in the sense that it is primarily God who gives it to us. Nor do we "have" it either, in the sense that it must not be invented by us. We must let ourselves fall, so to speak, into the communion of faith, of the Church. Believing is in itself a Catholic act. It is participation in this great certainty, which is present in the Church as a living subject.

Only in this way can we also understand Sacred Scripture in the diversity of an interpretation that develops for thousands of years. It is a Scripture because it is an element, an expression of the unique subject — the People of God — which on its pilgrimage is always the same subject. Of course, it is a subject that does not speak of itself, but is created by God — the classical expression is "inspired" — a subject that receives, then translates and communicates this word. This synergy is very important.

We know that the Koran, according to the Islamic faith, is a word given verbally by God without human mediation. The Prophet is not involved. He only wrote it down and passed it on. It is the pure Word of God.

Whereas for us, God enters into communion with us, he allows us to cooperate, he creates this subject, and in this subject his word grows and develops. This human part is essential and also gives us the possibility of seeing how the individual words really become God's Word only in the unity of Scripture as a whole in the living subject of the People of God.

Therefore, the first element is the gift of God; the second is the sharing in faith of the pilgrim people, the communication in the Holy Church, which for her part receives the Word of God which is the Body of Christ, brought to life by the living Word, the divine Logos.

Day after day, we must deepen our communion with the Holy Church and thus with the Word of God. They are not two opposite things, so that I can say: I am pro-Church or I am pro-God's Word. Only when we are united in the Church:

Do we belong to the Church.

Do we become members of the Church.

Do we live by the Word of God, which is the life-giving force of the Church.

And those who live by the Word of God can only live it because it is alive and vital in the living Church.

12. Eugenio Pacelli was born in Rome on March 2, 1876, and, on March 2, 1939, was elected pope and took the name of Pius XII. This great pope is shrouded in silence, and we are deeply indebted to this pontiff, who also had great love for Germany. We all truly hope he will soon be raised to the honor of the altars.

THE FIFTH QUESTION was on Pius XII. Thank you for your question. He was the pope of my youth. We all venerated him. As was rightly said, he deeply loved the German people; he also defended them in the great catastrophe after the War. And I must add that before he was nuncio in Berlin, he was nuncio in Munich, because at the outset there was no papal representation in Berlin. He was also really close to us.

This seems to me the opportunity to express gratitude to all the great popes of the last century. The century began with

St. Pius X, then Benedict XV, Pius XI, Pius XII, Blessed John XXIII, Paul VI, John Paul I, and John Paul II.

I believe that this is a special gift in such a difficult century with two world wars and two destructive ideologies: Fascism-Nazism and Communism. It was in this very century, which was opposed to the faith of the Church, that the Lord gave us a series of great Popes; hence, a spiritual inheritance that I would say historically strengthened the truth of the primacy of the Successor of Peter.

13. The Diocese of Rome is seeking the best way and a new approach to respond to the needs of today's families. Families must be given fresh vitality; they must be made the subject rather than the object of pastoral care. In our time, the family is threatened by relativism and indifference. Parents, engaged couples, and children must be assisted with catechesis and continuous guidance; they need priests expert in humanity who understand peoples' needs. Married couples must be encouraged to revive the grace of the sacraments.

THE NEXT QUESTION dedicated to the family was made by the parish priest of St. Sylvia. Here, I cannot but fully agree. Furthermore, during the *ad limina*[11] visits I always speak to bishops about the family, threatened throughout the world in various ways.

---

[11] Literally in Latin *ad limina apostolorum*: "at the thresholds of the apostles." Every five years all the world's diocesan bishops are required to come to Rome to report on the state of their dioceses and confer with the offices of the Holy See. This is the "*ad limina apostolorum*" visit because the bishops are also coming to the thresholds of the places where Sts. Peter and Paul are buried.

The family is threatened in Africa because it is difficult to find the way from "traditional marriage" to "religious marriage," because there is a fear of finality.

Whereas in the West the fear of the child is caused by the fear of losing some part of life, in Africa it is the opposite. Until it is certain that the wife will also bear children, no one dares to enter marriage definitively. Therefore, the number of religious marriages remains relatively small, and even many "good" Christians with an excellent desire to be Christians do not take this final step.

Marriage is also threatened in Latin America for other reasons, and is badly threatened, as we know, in the West. So it is all the more necessary for us as Church to help families, which are the fundamental cell of every healthy society.

Only in families, therefore, is it possible to create a communion of generations in which the memory of the past lives on in the present and is open to the future. Thus, life truly continues and progresses. Real progress is impossible without this continuity of life, and, once again, it is impossible without the religious element. Without trust in God, without trust in Christ who in addition gives us the ability to believe and to live, the family cannot survive.

We see this today. Only faith in Christ and only sharing the faith of the Church saves the family; and on the other hand, only if the family is saved can the Church also survive. For the time being, I do not have an effective recipe for this, but it seems to me that we should always bear it in mind.

We must therefore do all that favors the family: family circles, family catechesis, and we must teach prayer in the family. This seems to me to be very important: Wherever people pray together the Lord makes himself present with that power that can also dissolve "sclerosis" of the heart, that hardness of heart that, according to the Lord, is the real reason for divorce.

Nothing else, only the Lord's presence, helps us to truly relive what the Creator wanted at the outset and that the Redeemer renewed. Teach family prayer and thus invite people to pray with the Church and then seek all the other ways.

$$\smile$$

14. Hearing of a mother and some women religious who have helped priests through a crisis prompts me to ask: Why should not women also have a hand in governing the Church? Women often function charismatically, with prayer, or on a practical level, like St. Catherine of Siena who obtained the popes' return to Rome. It would be right to promote the role of women in institutions too, since their viewpoint, which is different from that of men, could help priests in decision making.

I NOW REPLY TO THE parochial vicar of St. Jerome's — I see that he is still very young — who tells us how much women do in the Church and for priests themselves.

I can stress that in the First Eucharistic Prayer, the Roman Canon, the special prayer for priests: *"Nobis quoque peccatoribus,"*[12] always makes a deep impression on me. Here, in this realistic

---

[12] In the First Eucharistic Prayer, or ancient Roman Canon, the priest asks God in his mercy to give a share of the reward He gave to the apostles and martyrs "also to us sinners." In the older form of Mass, the so-called "Tridentine" Mass as it was before the Council and now today since Benedict XVI derestricted its use by means of the Motu Proprio *Summorum Pontificum*, the priest would always say the Roman Canon silently. At *nobis quoque peccatoribus* however, he would speak these three words aloud and strike his breast as a sign of sorrow for sin.

humility of priests, precisely as sinners, we pray to the Lord to help us to be his servants. In this prayer for the priest, precisely only in this prayer, seven women appear who surround the priest. They show themselves to be the believing women who help us on our way. Each one of us has certainly had this experience.

Thus, the Church has a great debt of gratitude to women. And you have correctly emphasized that at a charismatic level, women do so much, I would dare to say, for the government of the Church, starting with women religious, with the Sisters of the great Fathers of the Church such as St. Ambrose, to the great women of the Middle Ages — St. Hildegard, St. Catherine of Siena, then St. Teresa of Ávila — and lastly, Mother Teresa. I would say that this charismatic sector is undoubtedly distinguished by the ministerial sector in the strict sense of the term, but it is a true and deep participation in the government of the Church also.

How could we imagine the government of the Church without this contribution, which sometimes becomes very visible, such as when St. Hildegard criticized the bishops or when St. Bridget offered recommendations and St. Catherine of Siena obtained the return of the popes to Rome? It has always been a crucial factor without which the Church cannot survive.

However, you rightly say: We also want to see women more visibly in the government of the Church. We can say that the issue is this: The priestly ministry of the Lord, as we know, is reserved to men, since the priestly ministry is government in the deep sense, which, in short, means it is the Sacrament [of Orders] that governs the Church.

This is the crucial point. It is not the man who does something, but the priest governs, faithful to his mission, in the sense that it is the Sacrament, that is, through the Sacrament it is Christ himself who governs, both through the Eucharist and in the other Sacraments, and thus Christ always presides.

However, it is right to ask whether in ministerial service — despite the fact that here Sacrament and charism are the two ways in which the Church fulfils herself — it might be possible to make more room, to give more offices of responsibility to women.

15. I am responsible for the rehabilitation of the victims of religious sects. I am grateful to you, Your Holiness, for your frequent denunciation of the harm they cause. Many simple people are unable to discover their tricks without help, like unfortunate travelers on the infamous road from Jerusalem to Jericho. Your Holiness, do you not think it is urgently necessary today to train Good Samaritans? Would not such preparation be good in the seminaries and in specific courses held at the university level and in the permanent formation of the clergy responsible for the care of souls?

I DID NOT QUITE UNDERSTAND the words of the eighth question. I more or less understood that today, "humanity" on the way from Jerusalem to Jericho falls among robbers. The Good Samaritan offers assistance with the Lord's mercy.

We can only emphasize that in the end, it is man who fell and who falls again and again into the hands of robbers, and it is Christ who heals us. We must and can help him, both in the service of love and in the service of faith, which is also a ministry of love.

16. The Feast of the Holy Patrons of my parish, the Holy Martyrs of Uganda, is celebrated on June 3. I praise God for this pastoral experience. May more people join in prayer in and for Africa.

THEN, THE MARTYRS OF UGANDA. Thank you for your contribution. You remind us of the African continent, which is the great hope of the Church.

In recent months I have received the majority of the African bishops on their *ad limina* visits. I found it very edifying and comforting to see bishops of a high theological and cultural standard. They are zealous bishops, truly enlivened by the joy of faith. We know that this Church is in good hands, but that she still suffers because the nations are not yet formed.

In Europe it was precisely through Christianity that, in addition to the ethnic groups that existed, the great bodies of nations, the great languages were formed, and thus communion of cultures and places of peace — although later, these great areas of peace, in opposition to one another, created a new sort of war that had previously not existed.

However, in many parts of Africa we still have this situation where there are above all dominant ethnic groups. The colonial power then imposed boundaries within which nations now have to develop. But there is still the difficulty of finding oneself in a great mass and of discovering, in addition to the ethnic groups, the unity of democratic government as well as the possibility of opposing forms of colonial abuse that continue. Africa still continues to be the object of abuse by the great powers, and many conflicts would not have taken this form if the interests of these great powers had not been behind them.

Thus, I have also seen how, in all this confusion, the Church with her Catholic unity is the great factor that unites in dispersion. In many situations, especially now, after the great war in the Democratic Republic of the Congo, the Church has remained the one reality that functions and makes life continue, which provides the necessary assistance, guarantees coexistence, and helps to find the possibility of creating one great solution.

In this sense, in these situations, the Church also carries out a service that replaces the political level, giving the possibility of living together and of rebuilding communion after destruction and of rebuilding, after the outburst of hatred, the spirit of reconciliation. Many people have told me that precisely in these situations; the Sacrament of Penance is of great importance as a force of reconciliation and must also be administered with this in view.

In a word, I wanted to say that Africa is a continent of great hope, of great faith, of moving ecclesial realities, of zealous priests and bishops. But it has always been a continent that, after the destruction we brought to it from Europe, needs our brotherly help. And this cannot but be born from faith that also creates universal love, over and above human divisions.

This is our great responsibility in this epoch. Europe has exported its ideologies, its interests, but has also exported, with the mission, the factor of healing. Today, we are especially responsible for having a zealous faith that is communicated, that wants to help others, that is aware that giving faith does not mean introducing an alienating power but means giving the true gift that human beings need precisely in order to be creatures of love.

=—

17. I see with concern the situation in Rome, especially the plight of young people and adolescents "on the fringe of humanity," many of whom do not go to church. I believe that priests, lay people, and religious should be closer to our faithful, especially youth, and we should put our charisms at the service of catechesis.

A LAST POINT WAS TOUCHED on by the Carmelite parochial vicar of St. Teresa of Ávila who has rightly revealed his worries to us.

A simple and superficial optimism that does not discern the great threats to youth, children, and families today would certainly be erroneous. We must perceive with great realism these threats that come into being wherever God is absent. We must be more and more aware of our responsibility so that God will be present and thus the hope and the ability to walk confidently towards the future.

=—

18. Adolescents are victims of today's "desert of love" and suffer appallingly from lack of love. They suffer from the fear of being lonely and misunderstood. Some priests also feel "inwardly dislocated." How can we be experts in "agape," in the fullness of love, in order to be able to make the total gift of ourselves to help them?

WE CAN TANGIBLY FEEL today all that you said about the problem of adolescents, their loneliness, and their being misunderstood by adults. It is interesting that these young people who seek closeness in discotheques are actually suffering from great loneliness and, of course, also from misunderstanding.

This seems to me, in a certain sense, an expression of the fact that parents, as has been said, are largely absent from the formation of the family. And mothers too are obliged to work outside the home. Communion between them is very fragile. Each family member lives in a world of his or her own: They are isolated in their thoughts and feelings, which are not united. The great problem of this time — in which each person, desiring to have life for himself, loses it because he is isolated and isolates the other from him — is to rediscover the deep communion which in the end can only stem from a foundation that is common to all souls, from the divine presence that unites all of us.

I think that the condition for this is to overcome loneliness and misunderstanding, because the latter also results from the fact that thought today is fragmented. Each one seeks his own way of thinking and living and there is no communication in a profound vision of life. Young people feel exposed to new horizons that previous generations do not share; therefore, continuity in the vision of the world is absent, caught up as it is in an ever more rapid succession of new inventions.

In ten years, changes have taken place that previously never occurred in 100 years. In this way worlds are really separated. I am thinking of my youth and of the "ingenuousness," if you will, in which we lived, in a society that was totally agricultural in comparison with contemporary society. We see that the world is changing at an ever-faster pace, so that also with these changes it is fragmented. Therefore, at a moment of renewal and change, the element of stability becomes even more important.

I remember when the conciliar Constitution *Gaudium et Spes*[13] was discussed. On the one hand, there was a recognition of the new, of newness, the "yes" of the Church to the new epoch with its innovations, its "no" to the romanticism of the past, a proper and necessary "no."

However, the Fathers — proof of this is also in the text — also said that in spite of this, in spite of the necessary willingness to move forward and even leave behind other things that were dear to us, there is something that does not change, because it is the human being himself, his being as a creature.

Man is not completely historical. The absolutizing of historicism, in the sense that man is only and always a creature, the product of a certain period, is not true. His nature as a creature exists, and it is precisely this that gives us the possibility to live through change and to retain our identity.

This is not an instant response to what we should do, but it seems to me that the first step should be to obtain the diagnosis. Moreover, why should this loneliness exist in a society that appears to be a society of the masses? Why should there be this lack of understanding in a society where everyone is seeking to understand one another, where communication is everything and where the transparency of all things to all people is the supreme law?

The answer lies in the fact that we see the change in our own world and do not sufficiently live that element that binds us all together, the element of our nature as creatures that becomes accessible and becomes reality in a certain history: The history of Christ, who is not against our nature as creatures

---

[13] Pastoral Constitution on the Church in the Modern World (Document of Vatican II).

but restores all that the Creator desired, as the Lord says about marriage.

Christianity precisely emphasizes history and religion as a historical event, an event in history starting with Abraham. Then, as a historical faith, after opening the door to modernity with its sense of progress and by constantly moving ahead, Christianity is at the same time a faith based on the Creator who reveals himself and makes himself present in a history to which he gives continuity, hence, communicability between souls.

Here too, therefore, I think that a faith lived in depth that is fully open to today but also fully open to God, combines the two things: respect for otherness and newness and the continuity of our being, communicability between people and between times.

The other point was: How can we live life as a gift? This is a question that we ask now, especially in Lent. We want to renew the option for life, which is, as I have said, an option not to possess ourselves but to give ourselves.

It seems to me that we can only do so by means of an ongoing conversation with the Lord and a conversation with one another. Also with *"correctio fraternal,"*[14] it is necessary to develop the gift of one's self more and more in the face of an ever-insufficient capacity to live.

But, it seems to me that we must also unite both things. On the one hand, we must accept our inadequacy with humility,

---

[14] "Fraternal correction" is an admonition given to a sinner out of charity to help him change his ways. We have an obligation under natural law to help people change. Christ himself also laid this down in Matthew 18:15. Great prudence must be used, however: we must be certain that the person really is sinning in a specific way; there must be a reasonable hope that the correction will do some good; we should not cause harm to ourselves by making the correction.

accept this "I" that is never perfect but always reaches for the Lord in order to arrive at communion with the Lord and with all people. This humility in accepting our own limitations is also very important.

Only in this way, on the other hand, can we also grow, develop, and pray to the Lord that he will help us not to tire along the way, also accepting humbly that we will never be perfect and accepting imperfections, especially in others. By accepting our own imperfections we can more easily accept those of others, allowing ourselves to be formed and reformed ever anew by the Lord.

19. Holy Father, I bring you the greetings of my confreres who work in secular hospitals, of the sick, and of healthcare workers. We ask you for a word of encouragement to help everyone be salt, light, and leaven in the healthcare sector.

NOW FOR HOSPITALS. Thank you for the greeting from the hospitals. I did not know of the mind-set that sees a priest carrying out his ministry in a hospital because he did something wrong. . . . I always thought that service to the sick and the suffering was a primary service of the priest, because the Lord came above all to be with the sick. He came to share our suffering and to heal us.

On the occasion of the *ad limina* visits of the African bishops, I always say that the two pillars of our work are education — that is, the formation of the human being which involves so many dimensions, such as education, learning, professionalism, the in-depth education of the person — and healing. The fundamental, essential service of the Church is therefore that of healing. All this is done precisely in the African countries: The Church offers healing. She presents people who help the sick, helps them to recover in body and soul.

It seems to me, therefore, that we should see the Lord himself as our model of the priesthood in order to heal, help, assist, and accompany people on their way towards recovery. This is fundamental to the Church's commitment; it is a fundamental form of love and, consequently, a fundamental expression of faith. Thus, it is also the central point in the priesthood.

20. Last September, I had the joy of taking part in an ecumenical meeting hosted by the Orthodox Patriarchate of Athens. It was a deeply enriching dialogue. I believe the clergy should avoid a conflictual attitude and establish a frank and serene dialogue with everyone.

THEN, I RESPOND to the parochial vicar of Holy Patrons of Italy Parish who has spoken to us of the dialogue with the Orthodox and of ecumenical dialogue in general.

In today's world situation, we see that dialogue at all levels is fundamental. It is even more important for Christians not to be closed in on themselves but open.

Precisely in relations with the Orthodox I see that personal relationships are fundamental. In doctrine, we are largely united on all the fundamental matters, but it is in doctrine that it seems very difficult to make any headway. But drawing close to one another in communion, in our common experience of the life of faith, is the way to recognize one another as children of God and disciples of Christ.

And this is my experience of at least 40 or almost 50 years. This is an experience of common discipleship, that we actually live in the same faith, in the same apostolic succession, with the same sacraments, and therefore also with the great tradition of prayer; this diversity and multiplicity of religious cultures, of the culture of faith, is beautiful.

To have this experience is fundamental, and it perhaps seems to me that the convinced opposition to ecumenism of some, of a part of the monks of Mount Athos, stems also from the lack of a visible, tangible experience that the other also belongs to the same Christ, to the same communion with Christ in the Eucharist.

So this is very important: We must tolerate the separation that exists. St. Paul says that divisions are necessary for a certain time and that the Lord knows why: To test us, to train us, to develop us, to make us more humble. But at the same time, we are obliged to move towards unity, and moving towards unity is already a form of unity.

21. Your encyclical Deus Caritas Est[15] *has deeply enlightened me, especially Part II on pastoral charity, since it invites us to practice charity directly, not to wait for the poor to come to us, but to reach out to them and do something concrete for them. However, priests find it very difficult to pass on the faith to the younger generations. Sometimes we feel somewhat let down by a young*

---

[15] "God Is Love."

parochial vicar, yet we went to the same seminary and are only a few years older. Are we expecting too much, or is there something lacking in our formation?

LET US NOW TURN to the spiritual director of the seminary. The first problem was the difficulty of pastoral charity. We live it on the one hand, but on the other, I would also like to say: Courage. The Church gives many thanks to God, in Africa but also in Rome and in Europe! She does so much, and so many people are grateful to her, both in the area of the pastoral care of the sick and in the pastoral care of the poor and abandoned. Let us continue courageously to seek to find the best paths together.

The other point was focused on the fact that priestly formation even between close generations seems to be a little different for many people, and this complicates the common commitment to the transmission of faith. I noted this when I was Archbishop of Munich.

When we entered the seminary, we all had a common Catholic spirituality that was more or less mature. Let us say that we had a spiritual foundation in common. Seminarians now come from very different spiritual experiences. I observed at my seminary that they live on different "islands" of spirituality that had difficulties communicating.

Let us thank the Lord especially because he has given so many new impulses to the Church and also so many new forms of spiritual life, of the discovery of the riches of the faith. It is necessary above all not to neglect the common Catholic spirituality that is expressed in the Liturgy and in the great Tradition of faith. This seems to me to be very important. This point is also important with regard to the Council.

We need not, as I said to the Roman Curia before Christmas, live the hermeneutic of discontinuity, but rather the hermeneutic of renewal, which is the spirituality of continuity, of going ahead in continuity. This seems to me to be very important also as regards the liturgy. Let me take a concrete example that came to me this very day with today's brief meditation.

The *"statio"*[16] of today, the Thursday after Ash Wednesday, is St. George. Corresponding to this soldier-saint, there were once two readings on two holy soldiers.

The first spoke of King Hezekiah, who was ill and condemned to death and who prayed to the Lord, weeping: "Give me a little more life!" And the Lord was good and granted him another seventeen years of life. Hence, a beautiful healing and a soldier who could once again conduct his activities.

The second is the Gospel that tells us of the official of Capernaum with his sick servant. We thus have two motives: that of the healing and that of the "militia"[17] of Christ, of the great fight.

Now, in today's liturgy, we have two totally different readings. We have the one from Deuteronomy: "Choose life," and the Gospel: "Take up your cross and follow Christ," which means it is not necessary to seek your own life but to give life, and this is one interpretation of what "choosing life" means.

---

[16] Relating to the station churches in Rome.

[17] Literally "military service" or "military spirit, courage." In English we have a phrase "to soldier on" in the face of difficulties. We all have a part to play according to our vocations for our immediate sphere of influence and for the whole Church, which in this life can be described as "the Church Militant." As his faithful disciples we are obedient to the Lord, who is our King and great Captain. The centurion who asks the Lord to heal his servant demonstrates an awareness of our different roles and parts to play in life as well as great faith that if we do our part as best we may, God will provide.

I must say that I have always loved the liturgy. I was truly in love with the Church's Lenten journey, with these "stational churches" and the readings linked to these churches: a geography of faith that becomes a spiritual geography of the pilgrimage with the Lord. And I was somewhat unhappy at the fact that they had taken from us this connection between the "station" and the readings.

Today, I see that these very readings are most beautiful and express the Lenten program: choosing life, that is, renewing the "yes" of Baptism, which is precisely, a choice of life. In this regard there is an intimate continuity, and it seems to me that we must learn from this that it is only a fraction between discontinuity and continuity.

We must accept newness but also love continuity, and we must see the Council in this perspective of continuity. This will also help us in mediating between the generations in their way of communicating the faith.

~

22. There is a great lack of hope in the world today and widespread secularism. Believing in the Church and with the Church means responding to it, seeking the only thing necessary [love], as you pointed out in the encyclical Deus Caritas Est. *Contemplation is the only way to understand and love others, a simple way to being more Christian.*

Lastly, the priest of the Vicariate of Rome ended with a word that I perfectly make my own so that with it we can conclude: becoming simpler. This seems to me to be a very beautiful program. Let us seek to put it into practice and thus we will be more open to the Lord and to people.

III. Questions Asked by the Youth of Rome

The following questions were asked by young people gath-ered in Rome at St. Peter's for an encounter with the Holy Father on April 6, 2006, in preparation for World Youth Day XXI.

23. Your Holiness, I am Simone from St. Bartholomew's Parish. I am 21 years old and am studying chemical engineering at "La Sapienza University" of Rome.

First of all, thank you for addressing to us the Message for the 21st World Youth Day on the topic of the Word of God that illuminates the human being's steps through life. In the face of anxieties and uncertainties about the future, and even simply when I find myself grappling with the daily routine, I also feel the need to be nourished by God's Word and to know Christ better in order to find answers to my questions.

I often wonder what Jesus would have done in my place in a specific situation, but I don't always manage to understand what the Bible tells me. Moreover, I know that the books of the Bible were written by different people in different ages, in any case, very distant from me. How can I understand that what I read is nevertheless the Word of God that calls my life into question?

TO BEGIN, I SHALL answer by stressing a first point: It must first of all be said that one must not read Sacred Scripture as one reads any kind of historical book, such as, for example, Homer, Ovid, or Horace; it is necessary truly to read it as the Word of God — that is, entering into a conversation with God.

One must start by praying and talking to the Lord: "Open the door to me." And what St. Augustine often says in his homilies: "I knocked at the door of the Word to find out at last what the Lord wants to say to me," seems to me to be a very important point. One should not read Scripture in an academic way, but with prayer, saying to the Lord: "Help me to understand your Word, what it is that you want to tell me in this passage."

A second point is: Sacred Scripture introduces one into communion with the family of God. Thus, one should not read Sacred Scripture on one's own. Of course, it is always important to read the Bible in a very personal way, in a personal conversation with God; but at the same time, it is important to read it in the company of people with whom one can advance, letting oneself be helped by the great masters of *"Lectio divina."*[18]

For example, we have many beautiful books by Cardinal Martini, a true master of *"Lectio divina,"* who helps us enter into the life of Sacred Scripture. Nevertheless, one who is thoroughly familiar with all the historical circumstances, all the characteristic elements of the past, always seeks to open the door to show that the words which appear to belong to the past are also words of the present. These teachers help us to understand better and also to learn how to interpret Sacred Scripture properly. Moreover, it is also appropriate in general to read it in the company of friends who are journeying with me, who are seeking, together with me, how to live with Christ, to find what life the Word of God brings us.

A third point: If it is important to read Sacred Scripture with the help of teachers and in the company of friends, traveling companions, it is particularly important to read it in the great company of the pilgrim People of God, that is, in the Church.

---

[18] A "divine" or "spiritual reading." This is a method of reading Scripture in a prayerful way, going back to the early Fathers of the Church. This way of attentive prayerful reading, which involves reflective "listening," aims to unite the readers more closely with God and to gain special insights in the content of the Word of God. The method usually involves a continuous reading of a text, broken into sections, at a set period of time, such as an hour, at a regular time and place each day. One reads a passage slowly several times, meditates on what it means for one's life, prays to God according to how one's heart is moved, and then listens contemplatively to what God might be saying.

Sacred Scripture has two subjects. First and foremost, the divine subject: It is God who is speaking. However, God wanted to involve man in his Word. Whereas Muslims are convinced that the Koran was verbally inspired by God, we believe that for Sacred Scripture it is "synergy" — as the theologians say — that is characteristic, the collaboration of God with man.

God involves his People with his Word, hence, the second subject — the first subject, as I said, is God — is human. There are individual writers, but there is the continuity of a permanent subject — the People of God that journeys on with the Word of God and is in conversation with God. By listening to God, one learns to listen to the Word of God and then also to interpret it. Thus, the Word of God becomes present, because individual persons die but the vital subject, the People of God, is always alive and is identical in the course of the millenniums: It is always the same living subject in which the Word lives.

This also explains many structures of Sacred Scripture, especially the so-called "rereading." An ancient text is reread in another book, let us say 100 years later, and what had been impossible to perceive in that earlier moment, although it was already contained in the previous text, is understood in-depth.

And it is read again, ages later, and once again other aspects, other dimensions of the Word are grasped. So it was that Sacred Scripture developed, in this permanent rereading and rewriting in the context of profound continuity, in a continuous succession of the times of waiting.

At last, with the coming of Christ and the experience of the Apostles, the Word became definitive. Thus, there can be no further rewriting, but a further deepening of our understanding continues to be necessary. The Lord said: "The Holy Spirit will guide you into depths that you cannot fathom now." Consequently, the communion of the Church is the living subject of Scripture. However, here too the principal subject is the Lord himself, who continues to speak through the Scriptures that we have in our hands.

I think that we should learn to do three things: To read it in a personal colloquium with the Lord; to read it with the guidance of teachers who have the experience of faith, who have penetrated Sacred Scripture; and to read it in the great company of the Church, in whose liturgy these events never cease to become present anew and in which the Lord speaks with us today. Thus, we may gradually penetrate ever more deeply into Sacred Scripture, in which God truly speaks to us today.

⌒⌒

24. Holy Father, I am Anna. I am 19 years old, I am studying literature, and I belong to the Parish of St. Mary of Carmel.

One of the problems we are constantly facing is how to approach emotional issues. We frequently find it difficult to love. Yes, difficult: Because it is easy to confuse love with selfishness, especially today when most of the media almost impose on us an individualistic, secularized vision of sexuality in which everything seems licit and everything is permitted in the name of freedom and individual conscience.

The family based on marriage now seems little more than a Church invention, not to speak of premarital relations, whose prohibition appears, even to many of us believers, difficult to understand or anachronistic.... Knowing well that so many of us are striving to live our emotional life responsibly, could you explain to us what the Word of God has to tell us about this?

THIS IS A VAST QUESTION, and it would certainly be impossible to answer it in a few minutes, but I will try to say something. Anna herself has already given us some of the answers. She said that today love is often wrongly interpreted because it is presented as a selfish experience, whereas it is actually an abandonment of self and thus becomes a self-discovery.

She also said that a consumer culture falsifies our life with a relativism that seems to grant us everything, but in fact completely drains us.

So let us listen to the Word of God in this regard. Anna rightly wanted to know what the Word of God says. For me it is a beautiful thing to observe that already in the first pages of Sacred Scripture, subsequent to the story of man's creation, we immediately find the definition of love and marriage.

The sacred author tells us: "Therefore a man leaves his father and his mother and clings to his wife, and they become one flesh," one life (cf. Gn. 2:24–25). We are at the beginning, and we are already given a prophecy of what marriage is; and this definition also remains identical in the New Testament. Marriage is this following of the other in love, thus becoming one existence, one flesh, therefore inseparable — a new life that is born from this communion of love that unites and thus also creates the future.

Medieval theologians, interpreting this affirmation that is found at the beginning of Sacred Scripture, said that marriage is the first of the seven sacraments to have been instituted by God already at the moment of creation, in Paradise, at the beginning of history and before any human history.

It is a sacrament of the Creator of the universe; hence, it is engraved in the human being himself, who is oriented to this journey on which man leaves his parents and is united to a woman in order to form only one flesh, so that the two may be a single existence.

Thus, the sacrament of marriage is not an invention of the Church; it is really "con-created" with man as such, as a fruit of the dynamism of love in which the man and the woman find themselves and thus also find the Creator who called them to love.

It is true that man fell and was expelled from Paradise, or, in other words, more modern words, it is true that all cultures are polluted by the sin, the errors of human beings in their history, and that the initial plan engraved in our nature is thereby clouded. Indeed, in human cultures we find this clouding of God's original plan.

At the same time, however, if we look at cultures, the whole cultural history of humanity, we note that man was never able to forget completely this plan that exists in the depths of his being. He has always known in a certain sense that other forms of relationship between a man and a woman do not truly correspond with the original design for his being.

And thus, in cultures, especially in the great cultures, we see again and again how they are oriented to this reality: monogamy, the man and the woman becoming one flesh. This is how a new generation can grow in fidelity, how a cultural tradition can endure, renew itself in continuity and make authentic progress.

The Lord, who spoke of this in the language of the prophets of Israel, said referring to Moses, who tolerated divorce: Moses permitted you to divorce "because of the hardness of your hearts." After sin, the heart became "hard," but this was not what the Creator had intended, and the Prophets, with increasing clarity, insisted on this original plan.

To renew man, the Lord — alluding to these prophetic voices that always guided Israel towards the clarity of monogamy — recognized with Ezekiel that, to live this vocation, we need a new heart; instead of a heart of stone — as Ezekiel said — we need a heart of flesh, a heart that is truly human.

The Lord "implants" this new heart in us at Baptism, through faith. It is not a physical transplant, but perhaps we can make this comparison. After a transplant, the organism needs treatment, requires the necessary medicines to be able to live with the new heart so that it becomes "one's own heart" and not the "heart of another."

This is especially so in this "spiritual transplant" when the Lord implants within us a new heart, a heart open to the Creator, to God's call. To be able to live with this new heart, adequate treatment is necessary; one must have recourse to the appropriate medicines so that it can really become "our heart."

Thus, by living in communion with Christ, with his Church, the new heart truly becomes "our own heart" and makes marriage possible. The exclusive love between a man and a woman, their life as a couple planned by the Creator, becomes possible, even if the atmosphere of our world makes it difficult to the point that it appears impossible.

The Lord gives us a new heart, and we must live with this new heart, using the appropriate therapies to ensure that it is really "our own." In this way we live with all that the Creator has given us, and this creates a truly happy life.

Indeed, we can also see it in this world, despite the numerous other models of life: There are so many Christian families who live with faithfulness and joy the life and love pointed out to us by the Creator, so that a new humanity develops.

Lastly, I would add: We all know that to reach a goal in a sport or in one's profession, discipline and sacrifices are required; but then, by reaching a desired goal, it is all crowned with success.

Life itself is like this. In other words, becoming men and women according to Jesus' plan demands sacrifices, but these are by no means negative; on the contrary, they are a help in living as people with new hearts, in living a truly human and happy life.

Since a consumer culture exists that wants to prevent us from living in accordance with the Creator's plan, we must have the courage to create islands, oases, and then great stretches of land of Catholic culture where the Creator's design is lived out.

~

25. Most Holy Father, I am Inelida. I am 17 years old, an assistant to the Scout Cub Master in the Parish of St. Gregory Barberigo, and I am studying at the Mario Mafai senior secondary art school.

In your Message for the 21st World Youth Day you said: "There is an urgent need for the emergence of a new generation of apostles anchored firmly in the Word of Christ" (L'Osservatore Romano, *English edition, March 1, 2006, p. 3). These are such forceful and demanding words that they are almost frightening.*

Of course, we also want to be new apostles, but could you explain to us in greater detail what in your opinion are the greatest challenges to face in our time, and how you imagine these new apostles should be? In other words, what does the Lord expect of us, Your Holiness?

WE ALL ASK OURSELVES what the Lord expects of us. It seems to me that the great challenge of our time — this is what the bishops on their *ad limina* visits tell me, those from Africa, for example — is secularization: That is, a way of living and presenting the world as *"si Deus non daretur, "* in other words, as if God did not exist.

There is a desire to reduce God to the private sphere, to a sentiment, as if he were not an objective reality. As a result, everyone makes his or her own plan of life. But this vision, presented as though it were scientific, accepts as valid only what can be proven.

With a God who is not available for immediate experimentation, this vision ends by also injuring society. The result is in fact that each one makes his own plan and in the end finds himself opposed to the other. As can be seen, this is definitely an unlivable situation.

We must make God present again in our society. This seems to me to be the first essential element: that God be once again present in our lives, that we do not live as though we were autonomous, authorized to invent what freedom and life are. We must realize that we are creatures, aware that there is a God who has created us and that living in accordance with his will is not dependence but a gift of love that makes us alive.

Therefore, the first point is to know God, to know him better and better, to recognize that God is in my life, and that God has a place.

The second point — if we recognize that there is a God, that our freedom is a freedom shared with others, and that there must consequently be a common parameter for building a common reality — the second point presents the question: What God? Indeed, there are so many false images of God, a violent God, etc.

The second point, therefore, is recognizing God who has shown us his face in Jesus, who suffered for us, who loved us to the point of dying, and thus overcame violence. It is necessary to make the living God present in our "own" lives first of all, the God who is not a stranger, a fictitious God, a God only thought of, but a God who has shown himself, who has shown his being and his face.

Only in this way do our lives become true, authentically human; hence, the criteria of true humanism emerge in society.

Here too, as I said in my first answer, it is true that we cannot be alone in building this just and righteous life but must journey on in the company of good and upright friends, companions with whom we can experience that God exists and that it is beautiful to walk with God; and to walk in the great company of the Church, which presents to us down the centuries God who speaks, who acts, who accompanies us.

Therefore, I would say: To find God, to find God revealed in Jesus Christ, to walk in company with his great family, with our brothers and sisters who are God's family, this seems to me to be the essential content of this apostolate of which I spoke.

26. Your Holiness, I am Vittorio. I am from the parish of St. John Bosco in Cinecittà. I am 20 years old and am studying educational sciences at the University of Tor Vergata. Once again, in your Message you invite us not to be afraid to respond to the Lord with generosity, especially when he suggests following him in the consecrated or priestly life.

You tell us that if we are not afraid, if we trust in him, then we will not be deceived. I am convinced that many of us, here or among those at home who are watching us this evening on television, are thinking of following Jesus in a life of special consecration, but it is not always easy to understand if this is the right path. Can you tell us how you yourself came to understand your vocation? Can you give us some advice so that we can really understand whether the Lord is calling us to follow him in the consecrated or priestly life?

AS FOR ME, I grew up in a world very different from the world today, but in the end, situations are similar.

On the one hand, the situation of "Christianity" still existed, where it was normal to go to church and to accept the faith as the revelation of God, and to try to live in accordance with his revelation; on the other, there was the Nazi regime, which loudly stated: "In the new Germany there will be no more priests, there will be no more consecrated life, we do not need these people; look for another career." However, it was precisely in hearing these "loud" voices, in facing the brutality of that system with an inhuman face, that I realized that there was instead a great need for priests.

This contrast, the sight of that antihuman culture, confirmed my conviction that the Lord, the Gospel, and the faith were pointing out the right path, and that we were bound to commit ourselves to ensuring that this path survives. In this situation, my vocation to the priesthood grew with me, almost naturally, without any dramatic events of conversion.

Two other things also helped me on this journey: Already as a boy, helped by my parents and by the parish priest, I had discovered the beauty of the liturgy, and I came to love it more and more because I felt that divine beauty appears in it and that heaven unfolds before us.

The second element was the discovery of the beauty of knowledge, of knowing God and Sacred Scripture, thanks to which it is possible to enter into that great adventure of dialogue with God which is theology. Thus, it was a joy to enter into this 1,000-year-old work of theology, this celebration of the Liturgy in which God is with us and celebrates with us.

Of course, problems were not lacking. I wondered whether I would really be able to live celibacy all my life. Being a man of theoretical and not practical training, I also knew that it was not enough to love theology in order to be a good priest, but that it was also necessary to be always available to young people, the elderly, the sick, and the poor: the need to be simple with the simple. Theology is beautiful, but the simplicity of words and Christian life is indispensable. And so I asked myself: Will I be able to live all this and not be one-sided, merely a theologian, etc.?

However, the Lord helped me, and the company of friends, of good priests and teachers especially helped me.

To return to the question, I think it is important to be attentive to the Lord's gestures on our journey. He speaks to us through events, through people, through encounters: It is necessary to be attentive to all of this.

Then, a second point, it is necessary to enter into real friendship with Jesus in a personal relationship with him and not to know who Jesus is only from others or from books, but to live an ever deeper personal relationship with Jesus, where we can begin to understand what he is asking of us.

And then, the awareness of what I am, of my possibilities: on the one hand, courage, and on the other, humility, trust, and openness, with the help also of friends, of Church authority and also of priests, of families: What does the Lord want of me?

Of course, this is always a great adventure, but life can be successful only if we have the courage to be adventurous, trusting that the Lord will never leave me alone, that the Lord will go with me and help me.

⟞⟝

27. *Holy Father, I am Giovanni, I am 17 years old, I am studying at "Giovanni Giorgi" technological and scientific secondary school in Rome, and I belong to Holy Mary Mother of Mercy Parish.*

I ask you to help us to understand better how biblical revelation and scientific theory can converge in the search for truth.

We are often led to believe that knowledge and faith are each other's enemies; that knowledge and technology are the same thing; that it was through mathematical logic that everything was discovered; that the world is the result of an accident, and that if mathematics did not discover the theorem — God, it is because God simply does not exist.

In short, especially when we are studying, it is not always easy to trace everything back to a divine plan inherent in the nature and history of human beings. Thus, faith at times vacillates or is reduced to a simple sentimental act.

Holy Father, like all young people, I too am thirsting for the truth: But what can I do to harmonize knowledge and faith?

THE GREAT GALILEO said that God wrote the book of nature in the form of the language of mathematics. He was convinced that God has given us two books: the book of Sacred Scripture and the book of nature. And the language of nature — this was his conviction — is mathematics, so it is a language of God, a language of the Creator.

Let us now reflect on what mathematics is: In itself, it is an abstract system, an invention of the human spirit that as such in its purity does not exist. It is always approximated, but as such is an intellectual system, a great, ingenious invention of the human spirit.

The surprising thing is that this invention of our human intellect is truly the key to understanding nature, that nature is truly structured in a mathematical way, and that our mathematics, invented by our human mind, is truly the instrument for working with nature, to put it at our service, to use it through technology.

It seems to me almost incredible that an invention of the human mind and the structure of the universe coincide. Mathematics, which we invented, really gives us access to the nature of the universe and makes it possible for us to use it.

Therefore, the intellectual structure of the human subject and the objective structure of reality coincide: The subjective reason and the objective reason of nature are identical. I think that this coincidence between what we thought up and how nature is fulfilled and behaves is a great enigma and a great challenge, for we see that, in the end, it is "one" reason that links them both.

Our reason could not discover this other reason were there not an identical antecedent reason for both.

In this sense it really seems to me that mathematics — in which as such God cannot appear — shows us the intelligent structure of the universe. Now, there are also theories of chaos, but they are limited because if chaos had the upper hand, all technology would become impossible. Only because our mathematics is reliable, is technology reliable.

Our knowledge, which is at last making it possible to work with the energies of nature, supposes the reliable and intelligent structure of matter. Thus, we see that there is a subjective rationality and an objectified rationality in matter that coincide.

Of course, no one can now prove — as is proven in an experiment, in technical laws — that they both really originated in a single intelligence, but it seems to me that this unity of intelligence, behind the two intelligences, really appears in our world. And the more we can delve into the world with our intelligence, the more clearly the plan of Creation appears.

In the end, to reach the definitive question I would say: God exists or he does not exist. There are only two options. Either one recognizes the priority of reason, of creative Reason that is at the beginning of all things and is the principle of all things — the priority of reason is also the priority of freedom — or one holds the priority of the irrational, inasmuch as everything that functions on our earth and in our lives would be only accidental, marginal, an irrational result — reason would be a product of irrationality.

One cannot ultimately "prove" either project, but the great option of Christianity is the option for rationality and for the priority of reason. This seems to me to be an excellent option, which shows us that behind everything is a great Intelligence to which we can entrust ourselves.

However, the true problem challenging faith today seems to me to be the evil in the world: We ask ourselves how it can be compatible with the Creator's rationality. And here we truly need God, who was made flesh and shows us that he is not only a mathematical reason but that this original Reason is also Love. If we look at the great options, the Christian option today is the one that is the most rational and the most human.

Therefore, we can confidently work out a philosophy, a vision of the world based on this priority of reason, on this trust that the creating Reason is love and that this love is God.

IV. Questions Asked by Priests of the Diocese of Albano

The following questions were asked by priests of the Diocese of Albano during an encounter with Pope Benedict XVI at Castel Gandolfo (the Papal Summer Residence) on August 31, 2006.

⟿

28.[19] *Our bishop, if briefly, has described to you the situation of our Diocese of Albano. We priests are fully integrated into this Church and experience all the relative problems and complexities. Young and old, we all feel inadequate. This is firstly because we are so few in comparison with the many needs, and we come from different backgrounds; we also suffer from a shortage of priestly vocations. That is why we sometimes feel discouraged. We try to patch things up here and there and are often forced to attend only to emergencies, without any precise projects. Seeing how much there is to do, we are tempted to give priority to "doing" and to neglect "being"; this is inevitably reflected in our spiritual life, our conversation with God, our prayer and our charity (love) for our brethren, especially those who are far away. Holy Father, what can you tell us about this? I am a certain age . . . but is it possible for these young confreres of mine to hope?*

DEAR BROTHERS, I WOULD LIKE first of all to offer you a word of welcome and thanks: Thanks to Cardinal Sodano for his presence, with which he expresses his love and care for this Suburbicarian Church; thanks to you, Your Excellency, for your words. In a few sentences, you have presented to me the situation of this diocese with which I was not so well acquainted. I knew that it was the largest of the suburbicarian dioceses, but I did not know that its population had increased to 500,000. Thus, I see a diocese full of challenges and difficulties but certainly also full of joy in the faith. And I see that all the issues of

---

[19] Question asked by Fr. Giuseppe Zane, Vicar "ad omnia," 83 years old.

our time are present: emigration, tourism, marginalization, agnosticism, but also a firm faith.

I have no claim to be, as it were, an "oracle" that could respond adequately to every question. St. Gregory the Great's words, which you quoted, Your Excellency, which everyone knows, *"infirmitatem suam,"*[20] also apply to the pope. Day after day, the pope too must know and recognize *"infirmitatem suam,"* his shortcomings. He must recognize that only in collaboration with everyone, in dialogue, in common cooperation, in faith as *"cooperatores veritatis"*[21] — of the Truth that is a Person, Jesus — can we carry out our service together, each one doing his share. This means that my answers will not be exhaustive but piecemeal. Yet, let us agree that actually it is only in unison that we can piece together the "mosaic" of a pastoral work that responds to the immense challenges.

I[22] have to say that each one of us has moments of discouragement in the face of all that needs to be done, and the limits of what, instead, can realistically be done. Once again, this also concerns the Pope. What must I do at this time for the Church,

---

[20] "His own weakness." Pope St. Gregory I, "the Great," wrote (*ep.* I.26) that he nearly declined accepting his election as Bishop of Rome, because of "his own weakness" in the face of such overwhelming challenges. He had a strong inclination to the monastic life of silence, study, and prayer, much like Pope Benedict himself. He was called away from his life as a monk to be Bishop of Rome. Gregory was Pope in a very difficult time when the Empire was falling to pieces. In the vacuum of power and social services, the Pope had to be both spiritual and secular ruler of Rome, seeing also to people's material needs. It was a daunting task for which he felt himself inadequate.

[21] "Coworkers of the truth," a phrase from 3 John 8. This was Joseph Ratzinger's motto on his coat-of-arms as Archbishop of Munich and as a Cardinal. This reveals the Pope's insight that no one person has a corner on the truth. We must strive together, each with his own gifts and role, with God's help and with Christ, who is Truth, as our starting point and goal.

[22] The pope refered to Cardinal Sodanno at this point "Cardinal Sodano, you said that our dear confrere, Fr. Zane, seems somewhat pessimistic."

with so many problems, so many joys, so many challenges that concern the universal Church? So many things happen, day after day, and I am unable to respond to them all. I do my part, I do all I can. I try to identify the priorities. And I am glad that I have so many good collaborators to help me. I can already say, here at this moment: I see every day the great amount of work that the Secretariat of State does under your wise guidance. And only with this network of collaboration, fitting myself and my own limited capacities into a broader reality, can I and dare I move ahead.

Therefore, naturally, a parish priest who is on his own sees even better that so many things still need to be done in this situation that you, Fr. Zane, have briefly described. And he can only do something to "patch things up," as you said, a kind of "first aid" operation, knowing that far more ought to be done.

I would say, then, that firstly, what is necessary for all of us is to recognize our own limitations, to humbly recognize that we have to leave most things to the Lord. Today, we heard in the Gospel the Parable of the Faithful Servant (cf. Mt. 24:42–51). This servant, the Lord tells us, gives food to the others at the proper time. He does not do everything at once but is a wise and prudent servant who knows what needs to be done in a specific situation. He does so humbly and is also sure of his master's trust. So it is that we must likewise do our utmost to be wise and prudent and to trust in the goodness of our "Master," the Lord, for in the end it is he himself who must take the helm of his Church. We fit into her with our small gift and do the best we can, especially those things that are always necessary: celebrating the sacraments, preaching the Word, giving signs of our charity and our love.

As for the inner life you mentioned, I would say that it is essential to our service as priests. The time we set aside for prayer is not time taken from our pastoral responsibility but is precisely pastoral "work"; it is also praying for others. In the "Common of Pastors," one reads as a typical feature of the good Pastor that *"multum oravit pro fratribus."*[23] This is proper to the Pastor, that he should be a man of prayer, that he should come before the Lord praying for others, even replacing others who perhaps do not know how to pray, do not want to pray or do not make the time to pray. Thus, it is obvious that this dialogue with God is pastoral work!

I would say further that the Church gives us, imposes upon us — but always like a good Mother — the obligation to make free time for God with the two practices that constitute a part of our duties: The celebration of Holy Mass and the recitation of the Breviary. However, rather than reciting it, this means putting it into practice by listening to the word which the Lord offers us in the Liturgy of the Hours.

It is essential to interiorize this word, to be attentive to what the Lord is saying to me with this word, to listen, then, to the comments of the Fathers of the Church or also of the Council in the Second Reading of the Office of Readings, and to pray with this great invocation, the Psalms, by which we are inserted into the prayer of all the ages. The people of the Old Covenant pray with us, and we pray with them. We pray with

---

[23] Literally, "He prayed much for the brethren." The Holy Father makes subtle use of the Latin preposition "pro," which is not merely "for" as in "on behalf of," but also possibly "in the place of." The priest, who carries out Christ's three-fold office to teach, govern and sanctify the people, acts as a mediator for the people with God. He prays in the Church both for himself and for God's people, and in place of the people even when they are not themselves praying as they ought.

the Lord, who is the true subject of the Psalms. We pray with the Church of all times. I would say that this time dedicated to the Liturgy of the Hours is precious time. The Church offers to us this freedom, this free space of life with God, which is also life for others.

Thus, it seems important to me to see that these two realities — Holy Mass truly celebrated in conversation with God and the Liturgy of the Hours — are areas of freedom, of inner life, an enrichment that the Church bestows upon us. In them, as I said, we do not find only the Church of all the ages but also the Lord himself, who speaks to us and awaits our answer. We thus learn to pray by immersing ourselves in the prayer of all times, and we also encounter the people. Let us think of the Psalms, of the words of the prophets, of the words of the Lord and of the apostles, let us think of the Fathers' comments.

Today, we have had St. Columban's marvelous comment on Christ, the source of "living water" from which we drink. In praying, we also encounter the suffering of the People of God today. These prayers remind us of daily life and guide us in the encounter with today's people. They enlighten us in this encounter, because we do not only bring to it our own small intelligence, our love of God, but we learn through this Word of God also to bring God to them. They expect this of us: that we bring them the "living water" of which St. Columban speaks today. The people are thirsty and try to satisfy this thirst with various palliatives. But they understand well that these diversions are not the "living water" that they need. The Lord is the source of "living water." But he says in chapter 7 of John that he who believes becomes a "river" because he has drunk from

Christ. And this "living water" (cf. Jn. 7:38) becomes a fountain of water in us, a source for others. In this way we seek to drink it in prayer, in the celebration of Holy Mass, in reading: We seek to drink from this source so that it may become a source within us. And we can respond better to the thirst of people today if we have within us the "living water," the divine reality, the reality of the Lord Jesus made flesh. Thus, we can respond better to the needs of our people.

This deals with the first question. What can we do? We always do all we can for the people — in the other questions, we will be able to return to this point — and we live with the Lord in order to respond to people's true thirst.

Your second question was: Is there any hope for this diocese, for this portion of the People of God that makes up this Diocese of Albano, and for the Church? I respond without hesitation: Yes! Of course we have hope: The Church is alive! We have 2,000 years of the Church's history with so much suffering and even so many failures: Let us think of the Church in Asia Minor and the great and flourishing Church in North Africa that disappeared with the Muslim invasion. Thus, parts of the Church can truly disappear, as St. John — or the Lord through John — said in the Book of Revelation: "I will come to you and remove your lampstand from its place, unless you repent" (Rev. 2:5). But, on the other hand, we perceive how the Church has re-emerged from so many crises with new youth, with a new freshness.

Actually, in the century of the Reformation, the Catholic Church seemed almost to have come to her end. This new current that declared: "Now the Church of Rome is finished," seemed to triumph. And we see that with the great saints, such as Ignatius of Loyola, Teresa of Ávila, Charles Borromeo, and others, that the Church was resurrected. In the Council of Trent, she found a new actualization and the revitalization of her doctrine. And she lived again with great vitality. Let us look at the age of the Enlightenment, when Voltaire said: "At last this ancient Church is dead, humanity is alive!" And instead, what happens? The Church is renewed.

The nineteenth century became the century of the great saints, of new vitality for a multitude of religious congregations, and faith is stronger than all the currents that come and go. And this also happened in the past century. Hitler once said: "Providence called me, a Catholic, to have done with Catholicism. Only a Catholic can destroy Catholicism." He was sure that he had all the means to be able at last to destroy Catholicism. Likewise, the great Marxist trend was convinced that it would achieve the scientific revision of the world and open doors to the future: The Church is nearing her end, she is done for! The Church, however, is stronger, as Christ said. It is Christ's life that wins through in his Church.

Even in difficult times when there is a shortage of vocations, the Word of the Lord lives forever. And he who, as the Lord himself said, builds his life on this "rock" of the Word of Christ, builds it well. Therefore, we can be confident. We also see new initiatives of faith in our day. We see that in Africa, despite all her problems, the Church has fresh new vocations, which is encouraging.

Thus, with all the differences of the historical prospect of today, we see — and not only see but believe — that the words of the Lord are spirit and life, they are words of eternal life. St. Peter said, as we heard last Sunday in the Gospel: "You have the words of eternal life; and we have believed, and have come to know, that you are the Holy One of God" (Jn. 6:68–69). And in looking at the Church today, together with all the suffering we see the Church's vitality, and we ourselves can also say: We have believed and have come to know that you offer us the words of eternal life, hence, a never-failing hope.

29.[24] In recent years, in harmony with the project of the Italian Bishops' Conference for the decade 2000–2010, we have been striving to implement a project for "integrated pastoral care." There are many difficulties. It is worth remembering at least the fact that many of us priests are still bound to a certain not particularly mission-oriented pastoral practice that seemed to have been consolidated; it was so closely bound to a context, as people call it, "of Christianity." On the other hand, many of the requests of a large number of the faithful themselves presume the parish to be a "supermarket" of sacred services. So this is what I would like to ask you, Your Holiness: Is integrated pastoral care only a question of strategy, or is there a deeper reason why we must continue to work along these lines?

I MUST CONFESS that I had to learn the term, "integrated pastoral care" from your question. However, I have understood its content: that we must strive to integrate in a single pastoral process both the different pastoral workers who exist today and the different dimensions of pastoral work. I would therefore distinguish the dimensions of the subjects of pastoral

---

[24] Question asked by Msgr. Gianni Macella, parish priest in Albano.

work and then attempt to integrate the whole into a single pastoral process.

In your question, you have explained that there is, shall we say, the "classic" level of work in the parish for the faithful who have stayed on — and who perhaps are also increasing — and give life to our parish. This is "classic" pastoral care, and it is always important. I usually make a distinction between continuous evangelization — because faith continues, the parish survives — and the new evangelization that seeks to be missionary, to supersede the limits of those who are already "faithful" and live in the parish or who, perhaps with a "reduced" faith, make use of parish services.

In the parish, it seems to me that we have three fundamental commitments that stem from the essence of the Church and the priestly ministry.

The first is sacramental service. I would say that Baptism, its preparation, and the commitment to giving continuity to the baptismal promises, already puts us in contact with those who are not convinced believers. It is not, let us say, a task of preserving Christianity, but rather an encounter with people who may seldom go to church. The task of preparing for Baptism, of opening the hearts of parents, relatives, and godparents to the reality of Baptism already can and should be a missionary commitment that goes beyond the boundaries of people who are already "faithful."

In preparation for Baptism, let us seek to make people understand that this sacrament is insertion into God's family, that God is alive, that he cares for us. He cares for us to the point that he took on our flesh and instituted the Church, which is his Body, in which he can, so to speak, put on new flesh in our society. Baptism is a newness of life in the sense that, as well as the gift of biological life, we need the gift of a meaning for life that is stronger than death and that will endure even when, one day, the parents are no longer alive. The gift of biological life is justified only if we can add the promise of a stable meaning, of a future that, also in future crises — which we cannot know — will give value to life so that it is worth living, worth being creatures.

I think that in the preparation for this sacrament or in conversation with parents who view Baptism with suspicion, we have a missionary situation. It is a Christian message. We must make ourselves interpreters of the reality that begins with Baptism.

I am not sufficiently familiar with the Italian rite.[25] In the classic rite, inherited from the ancient Church, Baptism begins with the question: "What do you ask of God's Church?" Today, at least in the German rite, the response is simply "Baptism." This does not adequately explain what it is that should be desired. In the ancient rite the answer was "faith": That is, a relationship with God, acquaintanceship with God. "Why do you ask for faith," the rite continues. "Because we wish for eternal life": We also want a safe life in future crises, a life that has meaning, that justifies being human. In any case, it seems to me that this dialogue should take place with the parents prior to Baptism. This is only to say that the gift of the Sacrament is

---

[25] The Holy Father is referring not so much to a different "rite" as if entirely different ceremonies are used in Italy or in Germany. This refers more to the options in the rite that are approved by the Church and customarily used in one place perhaps more than in another.

not merely a "thing," it is not merely "reifying" it, as the French say; it is missionary work.

Then there is Confirmation to prepare for at the age when people also begin to make decisions with regard to faith. Of course, we must not turn Confirmation into a form of "Pelagianism," almost as if in it one became Catholic by oneself, but rather into a blending of gift and response.

Finally, the Eucharist is Christ's permanent presence in the daily celebration of Holy Mass. It is very important, as I have said, for the priest, for his priestly life, as the real presence of the gift of the Lord.

We can now also mention marriage: Marriage too presents itself as a great missionary opportunity because today — thanks be to God — many people, even those who do not go to church often, still want to marry in church. It is an opportunity to make these young people face the reality of Christian marriage, sacramental marriage. This also seems to me a great responsibility. We see it in causes of the nullity of marriage, and we see it above all in the great problem of divorced and remarried people who want to receive Communion and do not understand why this is impossible. It is more than likely that when they said their "yes" before the Lord, they did not understand what this "yes" means. It is an identification with the "yes" of Christ, it means entering into the fidelity of Christ, hence, into the sacrament that is the Church and thus, into the Sacrament of Marriage.

I therefore think that preparation for marriage is a very important missionary opportunity for proclaiming the Sacrament of Christ once again in the Sacrament of Marriage, to understand this fidelity and thereby help people to understand the problem of those who are divorced and remarried.

This is the first and "classic" section of the sacraments that gives us the opportunity to meet people who do not go to church every Sunday: Hence, an opportunity for a truly missionary proclamation, for "integrated pastoral care."

The second section is the proclamation of the Word with the two essential elements: homily and catechesis.

In the Synod of Bishops last year, the fathers spoke a lot about the homily, emphasizing how difficult it is today to find a "bridge" between the Word of the New Testament, written 2,000 years ago, and our present day. I must say that historical and critical exegesis often does not give us sufficient help in drafting the homily. I notice it myself as I try to prepare homilies that actualize the Word of God: Or rather, given that the Word has an actuality in itself, that make people perceive, understand, this actuality. Historical-critical exegesis has much to tell us about the past, about the moment when the Word was born, about the meaning it had at the time of Jesus' apostles; but it does not always give us enough help in understanding that the words of Jesus, of the apostles, and also of the Old Testament are spirit and life: The Lord of the Old Testament also speaks today.

I think we have "to challenge" theologians — the Synod did so — to move ahead, to give parish priests greater help in preparing their homilies and in making the presence of the Word visible: The Lord speaks to me today and not only in the past.

In the last few days I have been reading the draft of the Post-Synodal Apostolic Exhortation. I was pleased to see that this "challenge" of preparing sample homilies has returned. In the end, the homily is prepared by the parish priest in his own context, for he speaks to "his" parish. But he needs help in understanding and in making understood this "present" of the Word that is never a Word of the past but of the "present."

Lastly, the third section: *Caritas,*[26] *diakonia.*[27] We are always responsible for the suffering, the sick, the marginalized, the poor. From the portrait of your diocese, I see that many are in need of our *diakonia,* and this is also always a missionary opportunity. Thus, it seems to me that the "classic" parish pastoral ministry transcends itself in all three sectors and is becoming missionary pastoral care.

I now move on to the second aspect of pastoral care, concerning both the agents and the work that is to be done. The parish priest cannot do it all! It is impossible! He cannot be a "soloist"; he cannot do everything but needs other pastoral workers. It seems to me that today, both in the movements and in Catholic Action, in the new communities that exist, we have agents who must be collaborators in the parish if we are to have "integrated" pastoral care.

I would like to say that for this "integrated" pastoral ministry it is important today that the other agents present are not only activated but are integrated in the work of the parish. The parish priest must not only "do," but also "delegate." The others must

---

[26] *"Caritas"* is Latin for "charity," the sacrificial love that is one of the theological virtues infused at Baptism and increased in the state of grace. Charity, as distinguished from lesser forms of love, always looks to the good of the other, for love of neighbor and love of God. "Caritas" is also the name of an international Catholic charitable organization. Pope Benedict wrote about this in his first encyclical *"Deus caritas est... God is love"* and in his Post-Synodal Exhortation *"Sacramentum Caritatis"* about the Eucharist and its liturgical celebration.

[27] *"Diakonia"* is Greek for "service" or "ministry" in the Church. It gives us the word "deacon," a minister especially concerned with the material goods of the Church and service of the poor.

learn to be really integrated in their joint work for the parish and, of course, also in the self-transcendence of the parish in a double sense: self-transcendence in the sense that parishes collaborate within the diocese because the bishop is their common pastor and helps coordinate their commitments; and self-transcendence in the sense that they work for all the people of this time and seek to reach out with the message to agnostics and to people who are searching. This is the third level, of which we have previously spoken at length.

It seems to me that the opportunities mentioned give us the chance to meet and to say a missionary word to those who do not come to the parish, have no faith, or have little faith. It is especially these new subjects of pastoral care and lay people who exercise the professions of our time, who must also take God's Word to areas often inaccessible to the parish priest.

Coordinated by the bishop, let us seek together to organize these different sectors of pastoral care, to activate the various agents and recipients of pastoral care in the common commitment: on the one hand, to encourage the faith of believers, which is a great treasure, and on the other, to reach out with the proclamation of the faith to all who are sincerely seeking a satisfying response to their existential questions.

30.[28] *Your Holiness, for the pastoral year that is about to begin, our diocese was asked by the bishop to pay special attention to the liturgy, in the theological dimension and in celebrative prac-*

---

[28] Question asked by Fr. Vittorio Petruzzi, parochial vicar in Aprilia.

tices. *The central theme for reflection at the residential weeks in which we shall be taking part in September is: "The planning and implementation of the proclamation in the liturgical year, in sacraments, and in sacramentals." As priests, we are called to celebrate a "serious, simple, and beautiful liturgy," to use a beautiful formula contained in the document "Communicating the Gospel in a Changing World" by the Italian bishops. Holy Father, can you help us to understand how all this can be expressed in the "ars celebrandi"*[29]*?*

ARS CELEBRANDI: Here too I would say that there are different dimensions. The first dimension is that the *celebratio*[30] is prayer and a conversation with God: God with us and us with God. Thus, the first requirement for a good celebration is that the priest truly enter this colloquy. In proclaiming the Word, he feels himself in conversation with God. He is a listener to the Word and a preacher of the Word, in the sense that he makes himself an instrument of the Lord and seeks to understand this Word of God that he must then transmit to the people. He is in a conversation with God because the texts of Holy Mass are not theatrical scripts or anything like them, but prayers, thanks to which, together with the assembly, I speak to God.

---

[29] This is a topic discussed at length during the Synod of Bishops of October 2005. Pope Benedict wrote about it at length in his Post-Synodal Exhortation *Sacramentum Caritatis*. It means "art of celebrating" the liturgy. This refers to the liturgical minister's self-awareness in his role, his style, understanding of what he is doing and why, so that the meaning of the rite itself is communicated through his words and actions. Especially important in Pope Benedict's discussion of *ars celebrandi* was the necessity for the priest (or bishop or deacon) never to impose his own personality on the rite so as to distort the content of the liturgy.

[30] Performance of a sacred function (e.g., the celebration of Mass).

It is important, therefore, to enter into this conversation. St. Benedict in his "Rule" tells the monks, speaking of the recitation of the Psalms, *"Mens concordet voci."*[31] The *vox,*[32] words, precede our mind. This is not usually the case: One has to think first, then one's thought becomes words. But here, the words come first. The sacred liturgy gives us the words; we must enter into these words, find a harmony with this reality that precedes us.

In addition, we must also learn to understand the structure of the liturgy and why it is laid out as it is. The liturgy developed in the course of two millenniums and even after the Reformation was not something worked out by simply a few liturgists. It has always remained a continuation of this ongoing growth of worship and proclamation.

Thus, to be well in tune, it is very important to understand this structure that developed over time and to enter with our *mens* into the *vox* of the Church. To the extent that we have interiorized this structure, comprehended this structure, assim-

---

[31] "The mind should be in harmony with the word."

[32] *Vox* in Latin is "word" or "voice" and it translates the Greek *"logos."* This gets into a complicated philosophical discussion of the way our minds form concepts, how we understand them through words, and how words then shape our concepts. Christ is the eternal Word, through whom all things were created. The word was made flesh and came into this world to reveal man more fully to himself (cf. John 1 and *Gaudium et Spes* 22). Our hearts and minds must be in harmony and be shaped by God's Word, both in Scripture and in the person of Christ, who speaks in the words of Scripture. In turn, our outward expressions in deed and word must be in concord with our inner minds and hearts, themselves in harmony with the divine Word. This dynamic process of being shaped in, by, and through the Word is like a "conversation" and that "conversation" becomes a whole way of life. St. Benedict may have been influenced not only by his own experience, but also by the writings of St. Augustine, who said: "What the voice pronounces should linger on in the heart." There is a reciprocal relationship between how we pray and what we believe (*lex orandi lex credendi*). So, we must allow ourselves to be shaped by our prayers, by the Church's "voice" in the liturgy, which rings with Christ's own voice.

ilated the words of the liturgy, we can enter into this inner consonance and thus not only speak to God as individuals, but enter into the "we" of the Church, which is praying. And we thus transform our "I" in this way, by entering into the "we" of the Church, enriching and enlarging this "I," praying with the Church, with the words of the Church, truly being in conversation with God.

This is the first condition: We ourselves must interiorize the structure, the words of the liturgy, the Word of God. Thus, our celebration truly becomes a celebration "with" the Church: Our hearts are enlarged, and we are not doing just anything but are "with" the Church, in conversation with God. It seems to me that people truly feel that we converse with God, with them, and that in this common prayer we attract others, in communion with the children of God we attract others; or if not, we are only doing something superficial.

Thus, the fundamental element of the true *ars celebrandi* is this consonance, this harmony between what we say with our lips and what we think with our heart. The "*Sursum corda,*"[33] which is a very ancient word of the Liturgy, should come before the Preface, before the liturgy, as the "path" for our speaking and thinking. We must raise our heart to the Lord, not only as a ritual response but as an expression of what is happening in this heart that is uplifted, and also lifts up others.

In other words, the *ars celebrandi* is not intended as an invitation to some sort of theater or show, but to an interiority that

---

[33] Literally "hearts upward," or as it is sometimes rendered "lift up your hearts." This is the exhortation of the priest during the preface to the Eucharistic Prayer in Holy Mass. The "dialogue" at the beginning of the preface has remained virtually the same since the early centuries of the Church.

makes itself felt and becomes acceptable and evident to the people taking part. Only if they see that this is not an exterior or spectacular *ars* — we are not actors! — but the expression of the journey of our heart that attracts their hearts too, will the Liturgy become beautiful, will it become the communion with the Lord of all who are present.

Of course, external things must also be associated with this fundamental condition, expressed in St. Benedict's words: "*Mens concordet voci*" — the heart is truly raised, uplifted to the Lord. We must learn to say the words properly.

Sometimes, when I was still a teacher in my country, young people had read the Sacred Scriptures. And they read them as one reads the text of a poem one has not understood. Naturally, to learn to say words correctly, one must first understand the text with its drama, with its immediacy. It is the same for the Preface and for the Eucharistic Prayer.

It is difficult for the faithful to follow a text as long as our Eucharistic Prayer. For this reason these new "inventions" are constantly cropping up. However, with constantly new Eucharistic Prayers one does not solve the problem. The problem is that this is a moment that also invites others to silence with God and to pray with God. Therefore, things can only go better if the Eucharistic Prayer is said well and with the correct pauses for silence, if it is said with interiority but also with the art of speaking.

It follows that the recitation of the Eucharistic Prayer requires a moment of special attention if it is to be spoken in such a way that it involves others. I believe we should also find opportunities in catechesis, in homilies, and in other circumstances to explain this Eucharistic Prayer well to the People of God so that they can follow the important moments — the account and the words of the Institution, the prayer for the living and the dead, the thanksgiving to the Lord, and the *epiclesis*[34] — if the community is truly to be involved in this prayer.

Thus, the words must be pronounced properly. There must then be an adequate preparation. Altar servers must know what to do; lectors must be truly experienced speakers. Then the choir, the singing, should be rehearsed: And let the altar be properly decorated. All this, even if it is a matter of many practical things, is part of the *ars celebrandi*.

But to conclude, the fundamental element is this art of entering into communion with the Lord, which we prepare for as priests throughout our lives.

~

31.[35] *Your Holiness, in the* Catechism of the Catholic Church *we read that "Holy Orders and Matrimony . . . are directed towards the salvation of others. . . . They confer a particular mission in the Church and serve to build up the People of God" (n. 1534). This seems to us truly fundamental, not only for our pastoral action but also for our way of being priests. What can we priests do to express this proposal in pastoral praxis and, according to what you yourself have just reaffirmed, to communicate positively the beauty of marriage which can still make the men*

---

[34] Greek for "invocation." This is the part of the Eucharistic Prayer during Mass when the priest begs God to send down the Holy Spirit upon the bread and wine on the altar so to change them through transubstantiation into the Body and Blood of Christ and so that the people will then benefit from them.

[35] Question asked by Fr. Angelo Pennazza, parish priest in Pavona.

and women of our time fall in love? What can the sacramental grace of spouses contribute to our lives as priests?

TWO TREMENDOUS QUESTIONS! The first one is: How is it possible to communicate the beauty of marriage to the people of today?

We see how many young people are reluctant to marry in church because they are afraid of finality; indeed, they are even reluctant to have a civil wedding. Today, to many young people and even to some who are not so young, definitiveness appears as a constriction, a limitation of freedom. And what they want first of all is freedom. They are afraid that in the end they might not succeed. They see so many failed marriages. They fear that this juridical form, as they understand it, will be an external weight that will extinguish love.

It is essential to understand that it is not a question of a juridical bond, a burden imposed with marriage. On the contrary, depth and beauty lie precisely in finality. Only in this way can love mature to its full beauty. But how is it possible to communicate this? I think this problem is common to us all.

For me, in Valencia,[36] it was an important moment not only when I talked about this, but when various families presented themselves to me with one or more children; one family was virtually a "parish," it had so many children! The presence and witness of these families really was far stronger than any words.

They presented first of all the riches of their family experience: How such a large family truly becomes a cultural treasure, an opportunity for the education of one and all, a

---

[36] The Holy Father is referring to the Fifth World Meeting of Families held in Valencia, Spain, on July 8–9, 2006.

possibility for making the various cultural expressions of today coexist, the gift of self, mutual help also in suffering, etc. But their testimony of the crises they had suffered was also significant. One of these couples had almost reached the point of divorcing. They explained that they then learned to live through this crisis, this suffering of the otherness of the other, and to accept each other anew. Precisely in overcoming the moment of crisis, the desire to separate, a new dimension of love developed and opened the door to a new dimension of life, which nothing but tolerating the suffering of the crisis could reopen.

This seems to me very important. Today, a crisis point is reached the moment the diversity of temperament is perceived, the difficulty of putting up with each other every day for an entire life. In the end, then, they decided: Let us separate. From these testimonies we understood precisely that in crises, in bearing the moment in which it seems that no more can be borne, new doors and a new beauty of love truly open.

A beauty consisting of harmony alone is not true beauty. Something is missing, it becomes insufficient. True beauty also needs contrast. Darkness and light complement each other. Even a grape, in order to ripen, does not need only the sun but also the rain, not only the day but also the night.

We priests ourselves, both young and old, must learn the need for suffering and for crises. We must put up with and transcend this suffering. Only in this way is life enriched. I believe that the fact the Lord bears the stigmata for eternity has a symbolic value. As an expression of the atrocity of suffering and death, today the stigmata are seals of Christ's victory, of the full beauty of his victory, and his love for us. We must accept, both as priests and as married persons, the need to put up with the crises of otherness, of the other, the crisis in which it seems that it is no longer possible to stay together.

Husbands and wives must learn to move ahead together, also for love of the children, and thus be newly acquainted with one another, love one another anew with a love far deeper and far truer. So it is that on a long journey, with its suffering, love truly matures.

It seems to me that we priests can also learn from married people precisely because of their suffering and sacrifices. We often think that celibacy on its own is a sacrifice. However, knowing the sacrifices married people make — let us think of their children; of the problems that arise; of the fears, suffering, illnesses, rebellion; and also of the problems of the early years when nights are almost always spent sleeplessly because of the crying of small children — we must learn our sacrifice from them, from their sacrifices. And at the same time we must learn that it is beautiful to mature through sacrifices and thus to work for the salvation of others.

Fr. Pennazza,[37] you correctly mentioned the Council, which says that marriage is a sacrament for the salvation of others: First of all for the salvation of the other, of the husband and of the wife, but also of the children, the sons and daughters, and lastly of the entire community. And thus, priesthood too matures in the encounter.

I then think that we ought to involve families. Family celebrations seem to me to be very important. On the occasion of celebrations it is right that the family, the beauty of families,

---

[37] Referring back to the questioner.

appear. Even testimonies — although they are perhaps somewhat too fashionable — can in some instances truly be a proclamation, a help for us all.

To conclude, I consider it very significant that in St. Paul's Letter to the Ephesians,[38] God's marriage with humanity through the Incarnation of the Lord is achieved on the Cross, on which is born the new humanity: the Church.

Precisely from these divine nuptials Christian marriage is born. As St. Paul says, it is the sacramental concretization of what happens in this great mystery. Thus, we must learn ever anew this bond between the Cross and the Resurrection, between the Cross and the beauty of the Redemption, and insert ourselves into this sacrament. Let us pray to the Lord to help us proclaim this mystery well, to live this mystery, to learn from married couples how they live it in order to help us live the Cross, so that we may also attain moments of joy and of the Resurrection.

32.[39] *Young people are the focus of a more decisive attention on the part of our dioceses and of the entire Church in Italy. The World Youth Days have led them to this discovery: There are a great many young people, and they are enthusiastic. Yet, our parishes in general are not adequately equipped to welcome them; parish communities and pastoral workers are not sufficiently trained to talk to them; the priests involved in the various tasks do*

---

[38] Ephesians 5:21–33.
[39] Question asked by Fr. Gualtiero Isacchi, Director of Diocesan Service for the Pastoral Care of Youth.

not have the time required to listen to them. They are remembered when they become a problem or when we need them to enliven some celebration or festivity. . . . How can a priest today express a preferential option for young people in view of his busy pastoral agenda? How can we serve young people based on their own scale of values instead of involving them in "our own things"?

I WOULD LIKE FIRST of all to stress what you have said. On the occasion of the World Youth Days and at other events — as recently, on the Eve of Pentecost[40] — it appears that young people are also in search of God. The young want to see whether God exists and what God tells us. Consequently, there is a certain willingness, in spite of all the difficulties of our time. An enthusiasm also exists. Therefore, we must do all we can to try to keep alive this flame that shows itself on occasions such as the World Youth Days.

What shall we do? This is our common question. I think that precisely here, an "integrated pastoral care" should be put into practice, for in fact not every parish priest can cope adequately with youth. He therefore needs a pastoral apostolate that transcends the limits of the parish and that also transcends the limits of the priest's work; a pastoral apostolate that involves numerous pastoral workers.

It seems to me that under the bishop's coordination, a way should be found, on the one hand, to integrate young people into the parish so that they may be the leaven of parish life; and on the other, also to obtain for these youth the help of extra-parochial personnel. These two things must go hand-in-hand.

---

[40] The Holy Father is referring to his encounter with the ecclesial communities and new movements at St. Peter's on the Vigil of Pentecost, June 3, 2006.

It is necessary to suggest to young people that not only in the parish but also in various contexts they must integrate themselves into the life of the dioceses so as to meet subsequently in the parish; so it is necessary to encourage all initiatives along these lines.

I think that volunteer experience is very important nowadays. It is vital not to leave young people to the mercy of discos but to have useful tasks for them to do in which they see they are necessary; realize that they can do something good. By feeling this impulse to do something useful for humanity, for someone, for a group, young people also become aware of this incentive to strive to find the "track" of a positive commitment, of a Christian ethic.

It seems to me very important that young people truly find tasks that demonstrate that they are needed, that guide them on the way of a positive service of assistance inspired by Christ's love for men and women, so that they themselves seek the sources from which to draw strength and commitment.

Another experience is offered by the prayer groups where, in their own youthful context, the young learn to listen to the Word of God, to learn the Word of God, and to enter into contact with God. This also means learning the common form of prayer, the liturgy, which at first sight might perhaps seem rather inaccessible to them. They learn that the Word of God exists and seeks us out, despite all the distance of the times, and speaks to us today. We offer to the Lord the fruit of the earth and of the work of our hands, and we find it transformed into a gift of God. We speak as children to the Father, and we then receive the gift of the Lord himself. We receive the mission to go out into the world with the gift of his Presence.

It would also be useful to have liturgy schools that young people could attend. Moreover, opportunities for young people to present and introduce themselves are vital. I heard that here in Albano a play on the life of St. Francis was performed. Committing oneself in this sense means desiring to penetrate the personality of St. Francis, of his time, and thereby widening one's own personality. It is only an example, something apparently fairly unusual. It can be a lesson to broaden the personality, to enter into a context of Christian tradition, to reawaken the thirst for a better knowledge of the sources from which this saint drew. He was not only an environmentalist or a pacifist. He was above all a convert.

I read with great pleasure that Bishop Sorrentino of Assisi, precisely to obviate this "abuse" of the figure of St. Francis, on the occasion of the eighth centenary of his conversion wished to establish a "Year of Conversion" to see what the true "challenge" is. Perhaps we can all animate youth a little to make the meaning of conversion understood by also finding a link with the figure of St. Francis and seeking a route that broadens life. Francis was first a kind of "playboy." He then felt that this was not enough. He heard the Lord's voice: "Rebuild my House." Little by little, he came to understand what "building the House of the Lord" means.

I do not, therefore, have very practical answers, because I find myself facing a mission where I already find young people gathered, thanks be to God. But it seems to me that one ought to make use of all the possibilities offered today by the movements, associations, and volunteer groups and in other activities for youth. It is also necessary to present young people to the parish so that it sees who the young people are. Vocations' promotion is necessary. The whole thing must be coordinated by the bishop. It seems to me that pastoral workers are found through the same authentic cooperation of young people who are training. And thus, it is possible to open the way to conversion, to the joy that God exists and is concerned about us, that we have access to God and can help others "rebuild his House."

It seems to me that this, finally, is our mission, sometimes difficult, but in the end very beautiful: To "build God's House" in the contemporary world.

Thank you for your attention, and I ask you to forgive me for my disconnected answers. Let us collaborate so that "God's House" in our time will grow and many young people will find the path of service to the Lord.

V. Questions Asked by Priests of the Diocese of Rome, Part 2

The following questions were asked by priests of the Diocese of Rome during an encounter with Pope Benedict XVI at St. Peter's on February 22, 2007.

33. The first question was addressed to the Holy Father by Msgr. Pasquale Silla, Rector at the Shrine of Santa Maria del Divino Amore at Castel di Leva, not far from Rome. Msgr. Silla recalled Benedict XVI's visit to the Shrine on May 1, 2006, and his request to the parish community for powerful prayer for the Bishop of Rome and his collaborators, as well as for the priests and faithful of the diocese. In response to this request, the community of Our Lady of Divine Love attempted to give the best possible quality to prayer in all its forms, especially liturgical prayer: One of the results of this commitment is the Perpetual Adoration of the Eucharist that was to begin at the Shrine in March 2007. In the field of charity, the Shrine is concentrating on broadening its outreach, especially in the area of welfare for minors, families, and the elderly. In this perspective, Msgr. Silla asked Pope Benedict XVI for practical instructions to enable the Shrine to play an increasingly effective role in the diocese.

I WOULD LIKE FIRST of all to say that I am glad and happy to feel here that I am truly the bishop of a large diocese. The Cardinal Vicar said that you are expecting light and comfort. And I must say that to see so many priests of all generations is light and comfort to me. Above all, I have already learned something from the first question, and to my mind this is another essential element of our meeting. Here I can hear the actual living voices of parish priests and their pastoral experiences; thus, above all I can learn about your concrete situation, your queries, your experiences, and your difficulties, and live them not only in the abstract but in authentic dialogue with real parish life.

I now come to the first question. It seems to me, basically, that you have also supplied the answer as to what this Shrine can do. . . . I know that this Marian shrine is the one best loved by the people of Rome. During the several visits I have paid to the ancient shrine, I also felt the age-old devotion. One senses the presence of the prayer of generations, and one can almost tangibly feel Our Lady's motherly presence.

In the encounter with Mary, it is truly possible to experience an encounter with the centuries-old Marian devotion as well as with the desires, needs, sufferings, and joys of the generations. Thus, this shrine, visited by people with their hopes, questions, requests, and sufferings, is an essential factor for the Diocese of Rome.

We are seeing more and more that shrines are a source of life and faith in the universal Church — hence, also in the Church of Rome. In my country, I had the experience of making pilgrimages on foot to our national Shrine of Altötting. It is an important popular mission.

Young people in particular go there. As pilgrims walking for three days, they experience the atmosphere of prayer and an examination of conscience and rediscover, as it were, their Christian awareness of the faith. These three days of pilgrimage on foot are days of confession and prayer, they are a true journey towards Our Lady, towards the family of God, and also towards the Eucharist.

Pilgrims go on foot to Our Lady, and with Our Lady they go to the Lord, to the Eucharistic encounter, preparing themselves for interior renewal with confession. They live anew the Eucharistic reality of the Lord who gives himself, just as Our

Lady gave her own flesh to the Lord, thereby opening the door to the Incarnation.

Our Lady gave her flesh for the Incarnation and thereby made possible the Eucharist, where we receive the Flesh that is Bread for the world. In going to the encounter with Our Lady, young people themselves learn to offer their own flesh, their daily life, so that it may be given over to the Lord. And they learn to believe and little by little to say "yes" to the Lord.

I would therefore say, to return to the question, that the Shrine as such, as a place of prayer, confession, and the celebration of the Eucharist, provides a great service in the Church today for the Diocese of Rome. I therefore think that the essential service, of which, moreover, you have spoken in practical terms, is precisely that of providing a place of prayer, of sacramental life, and of a life of practiced charity.

If I have understood correctly, you spoke of four dimensions of prayer. The first is personal. And here Mary shows us the way. St. Luke says twice that the Virgin Mary "kept all these things, pondering them in her heart" (Lk. 2:19; cf. Lk. 2:51). She was a person in conversation with God, with the Word of God and also with the events through which God spoke to her.

The *Magnificat*[41] is a "fabric" woven of words from Sacred Scripture. It shows us how Mary lived in a permanent conversation with the Word of God, and thus with God himself. Then of course, in life with the Lord, she was also always in conversation with Christ, with the Son of God, and with the Trinitarian God.

---

[41] Luke 1:46–56, Canticle of Mary that is prayed at Evening prayer every night. The word Magnificat is the first word of the first verse in Latin *Magnificat anima meum Dominum*, "My soul magnifies the Lord."

Therefore, let us learn from Mary and speak personally with the Lord, pondering and preserving God's words in our lives and hearts so that they may become true food for each one of us. Thus, Mary guides us at a school of prayer in personal and profound contact with God.

The second dimension you mentioned is liturgical prayer. In the Liturgy, the Lord teaches us to pray, first of all giving us his Word, then introducing us through the Eucharistic Prayer to communion with the mystery of his life, the Cross, and the Resurrection.

St. Paul once said we do not even know what to ask for: "We do not know how to pray as we ought" (Rom. 8:26); we do not know how to pray or what to say to God. God, therefore, has given us words of prayer in the Psalter, in the important prayers of the Sacred Liturgy, and precisely in the Eucharistic liturgy itself. Here, he teaches us how to pray.

We enter into the prayer that was formed down the centuries under the inspiration of the Holy Spirit, and we join in Christ's conversation with the Father. Thus, the liturgy, above all, is prayer: first listening and then a response, in the Responsorial Psalm, in the prayer of the Church, and in the great Eucharistic Prayer. We celebrate it well if we celebrate it with a "prayerful" attitude, uniting ourselves with the mystery of Christ and his exchange as Son with the Father.

If we celebrate the Eucharist in this way, first as listening and then as a response, hence, as prayer, using the words pointed out to us by the Holy Spirit, then we are celebrating it well. And through our prayer in common, people are attracted to joining the ranks of God's children.

The third dimension is that of popular piety. An important document of the Congregation for Divine Worship and the Discipline of the Sacraments[42] speaks of this popular piety and tells us how to "guide it." Popular piety is one of our strengths because it consists of prayers deeply rooted in people's hearts. These prayers even move the hearts of people who are somewhat cut off from the life of the Church and who have no special understanding of faith.

All that is required is to "illuminate" these actions and "purify" this tradition so that it may become part of the life of the Church today.

Then comes Eucharistic Adoration. I am very grateful because Eucharistic Adoration is being increasingly renewed. During the Synod on the Eucharist, the bishops talked a great deal about their experiences, of how new life is being restored to communities with this adoration, and also with nocturnal adoration, and how, precisely in this way, new vocations are also born.

I can say that I will shortly be signing the Post-Synodal Apostolic Exhortation on the Eucharist,[43] which will then be available to the Church. It is a document offered precisely for meditation. It will be a help in the liturgical celebration as well as in personal reflection, in the preparation of homilies, and in the celebration of the Eucharist. And it will also serve to guide, enlighten, and revitalize popular piety.

---

[42] *Directory on Popular Piety and the Liturgy: Principles and Guidelines*, Congregation for the Divine Worship and the Discipline of the Sacraments, Vatican, December 2001.

[43] The Holy Father signed the Post-Synodal Apostolic Exhortation *Sacramentum Caritatis* "On the Eucharist as the Source and Summit of the Church's Life and Mission" on February 22, 2007.

Lastly, you spoke to us of the Shrine as a place of *caritas*.[44] I think this is very logical and necessary. A little while ago I read what St. Augustine said in Book X of his *Confessions*:

> "I was tempted, and I now understand that it was a temptation to enclose myself in contemplative life, to seek solitude with you, O Lord; but you prevented me, you plucked me from it and made me listen to St. Paul's words: 'Christ died for us all. Consequently, we must die with Christ and live for all.' I understood that I cannot shut myself up in contemplation; you died for us all. Therefore, with you, I must live for all and thus practice works of charity. True contemplation is expressed in works of charity. Therefore, the sign for which we have truly prayed, that we have experienced in the encounter with Christ, is that we exist 'for others.'"

This is what a parish priest must be like. And St. Augustine was a great parish priest. He said:

> "In my life I also always longed to spend my life listening to the Word in meditation, but now — day after day, hour after hour — I must stand at the door where the bell is always ringing, I must comfort the afflicted, help the poor, reprimand those who are quarrelsome, create peace, and so forth."

St. Augustine lists all the tasks of a parish priest, for at that time the bishop was also what the *Qadi*[45] in Islamic countries is today. With regard to problems of civil law, let us say, he was the

---

[44] Literally "love" or "charity."
[45] A Muslim judge who rules in accordance with religious laws.

judge of peace: He had to encourage peace between the litigants. He therefore lived a life that for him, a contemplative, was very difficult. But he understood this truth: Thus, I am with Christ; in existing "for others," I am in the Crucified and Risen Lord.

I think this is a great consolation for parish priests and Bishops. Even if little time is left for contemplation, in being "for others," we are with the Lord.

You spoke of other concrete elements of charity that are very important. They are also a sign for our society, in particular for children, for the elderly, for the suffering. I therefore believe that with these four dimensions of life, he has given us the answer to your question: What should we do at our Shrine?

⌒

34. Fr. Maurizio Secondo Mirilli, parochial vicar of Santa Bernadette Soubirous Parish and head of the Diocesan Youth Program, emphasized the demanding task incumbent on priests in their mission to instill faith in the new generations. Fr. Mirilli asked the pope for a word of guidance on how to transmit the joy of the Christian faith to youth, especially in the face of today's cultural challenges, and also asked him to point out the priority topics on which to focus in order to help young men and women to encounter Christ in practice.

THANK YOU FOR YOUR WORK for teenagers. We know that the young really must be a priority of our pastoral work because they dwell in a world far from God. And in our cultural context it is not easy to encounter Christ, the Christian life, and the faith life.

Young people require so much guidance if they are truly to find this path. I would say — even if I unfortunately live rather far away from them and so cannot provide very practical instructions — that the first element is, precisely and above all, guidance. They must realize that living the faith in our time is possible, that it is not a question of something obsolete but rather, that it is possible to live as Christians today and so to find true goodness.

I remember an autobiographical detail in St. Cyprian's writings:

> "I lived in this world of ours totally cut off from God because the divinities were dead and God was not visible. And in seeing Christians I thought: It is an impossible life, this cannot be done in our world! Then, however, meeting some of them, joining their company, and letting myself be guided in the catechumenate, in this process of conversion to God, I gradually understood: It is possible! And now I am happy at having found life. I have realized that the other was not life, and to tell the truth, even beforehand, I knew that that was not true life."

It seems to me to be very important that the young find people — both of their own age and older — in whom they can see that Christian life today is possible, and also reasonable and feasible. I believe there are doubts about both these elements: about its feasibility, because the other paths are very distant from the Christian way of life, and about its reasonableness, because at first glance it seems that science is telling us quite different things and that it is therefore impossible to mark out a reasonable route towards faith in order to show that it is something attuned to our time and our reason.

Thus, the first point is experience, which also opens the door to knowledge. In this regard, the "catechumenate" lived in a new way — that is, as a common journey through life, a common experience of the possibility of living in this way — is of paramount importance.

Only if there is a certain experience can one also understand. I remember a piece of advice that Pascal gave to a nonbeliever friend. He told him: "Try to do what a believer does, then you will see from this experience that it is all logical and true."

I would say that one important aspect is being shown to us at this very moment by Lent. We cannot conceive of immediately living a life that is 100 percent Christian without doubts and without sins. We have to recognize that we are journeying on, that we must and can learn, and also, gradually, that we must convert. Of course, fundamental conversion is a definitive act. But true conversion is an act of life that is achieved through the patience of a lifetime. It is an act in which we must not lose trust and courage on the way.

We must recognize exactly this: We cannot make ourselves perfect Christians from one moment to the next. Yet, it is worth going ahead, being true to the fundamental option, so to speak, then firmly persevering in a process of conversion that sometimes becomes difficult.

Indeed, it can happen that I feel discouraged so that I am in a state of crisis and want to give up everything instantly. We should not allow ourselves to give up immediately, but should take heart and start again. The Lord guides me, the Lord is generous, and with his forgiveness I make headway, also becoming generous to others. Thus, we truly learn love for our neighbor and Christian life, which implies this perseverance in forging ahead.

As for the important topics, I would say that it is important to know God. The subject "God" is essential. St. Paul says in his Letter to the Ephesians: "Remember that you were at that time... having no hope and without God.... But now in Christ Jesus you who once were far off have been brought near" (Eph. 2:12–13). Thus, life has a meaning that guides me even through difficulties.

It is therefore necessary to return to God the Creator, to the God who is creative reason, and then to find Christ, who is the living Face of God. Let us say that here there is a reciprocity. On the one hand, we have the encounter with Jesus, with this human, historical, and real figure; little by little, he helps me to become acquainted with God; and on the other, knowing God helps me understand the grandeur of Christ's mystery which is the Face of God.

Only if we manage to grasp that Jesus is not a great prophet or a world religious figure but that he is the Face of God, that he is God, have we discovered Christ's greatness and found out who God is. God is not only a distant shadow, the "primary Cause," but he has a Face. His is the Face of mercy, the Face of pardon and love, the Face of the encounter with us. As a result, these two topics penetrate each other and must always go together.

Then of course, we have to realize that the Church is our vital traveling companion on our journey. In her, the Word of God lives on, and Christ is not only a figure of the past but is present. We must therefore rediscover sacramental life, sacramental forgiveness, the Eucharist, and Baptism as a new birth.

On the Easter Vigil, in his last mystagogical catechesis, St. Ambrose said: "Until now we have spoken of moral topics; it is now time to speak of the Mystery." He offered guidance in moral experience, in the light of God of course, but that then opens to the mystery. I believe that today these two things must penetrate each other: A journey with Jesus who increasingly unfolds the depths of his mystery. Thus, one learns to live as a Christian, one learns the importance of forgiveness and the greatness of the Lord who gives himself to us in the Eucharist.

On this journey, we are naturally accompanied by the saints. Despite their many problems, they lived and were true and living "interpretations" of Sacred Scripture. Each person has his saint from whom he can best learn what living as a Christian means. There are the saints of our time in particular, and of course there is always Mary, who remains the Mother of the Word. Rediscovering Mary helps us to make progress as Christians and to come to know the Son.

35. Fr. Franco Incampo, rector of the Church of Santa Lucia del Gonfalone, presented his experience of the integral interpretation of the Bible, on which his community has embarked together with the Waldensian Church. "We have set ourselves to listen to the Word," he said. "It is an extensive project. What is the value of the Word in the ecclesial community? Why are we so unfamiliar with the Bible? How can we further knowledge of the Bible so that the Word will also train the community to have an ecumenical approach?"

YOU CERTAINLY HAVE a more practical experience of how to do this. I can say in the first place that we will soon be celebrating the Synod on the Word of God.[46] I have already been able to

---

[46] The synod is scheduled to take place at the Vatican on October 5–26, 2008.

look at the *Lineamenta*[47] worked out by the Synod Council and I think that the various dimensions of the Word's presence in the Church appear clearly in it.

The Bible as a whole is of course enormous; it must be discovered little by little, for if we take the individual parts on their own, it is often hard to understand that this is the Word of God: I am thinking of certain sections of the Book of Kings with the Chronicles, with the extermination of the peoples who lived in the Holy Land. Many other things are difficult.

Even Qoheleth[48] can be taken out of context and prove extremely difficult: It seems to theorize desperation, because nothing is lasting and even the "preacher" dies in the end, together with the foolish.[49]

To my mind, a preliminary point would be to read Sacred Scripture in its unity and integrity. Its individual parts are stages on a journey and only by seeing them as a whole, as a single journey where each section explains the other, can we understand this.

Let us stay, for example, with Qoheleth. First, there was the word of wisdom according to which the good also live well: That is, God rewards those who are good. And then comes Job, and one sees that it is not like this and that it is precisely those who are righteous who suffer the most. Job seems truly to have been forgotten by God.

Then come the Psalms of that period where it is said: But what does God do? Atheists and the proud have a good life,

---

[47] Latin for "marks" or "sketches" as if with chalk. This has come to refer to the drafts or "talking points," outlines for the discussion of an upcoming meeting sent out to the participants ahead of time.

[48] Hebrew for "the preacher" in the Book of Ecclesiastes.

[49] The Holy Father commented to the clergy present on this point, "We had the Reading from it in the Breviary just now."

they are fat and well-nourished, they laugh at us and say: But where is God? They are not concerned with us, and we have been sold like sheep for slaughter. What do you have to do with us, why is it like that?

The time comes when Qoheleth asks: But what does all this wisdom amount to? It is almost an existentialist book, in which it is said: "All is vanity." This first journey does not lose its value but opens onto a new perspective that leads in the end to the Cross of Christ, "the Holy One of God," as St. Peter said in the sixth chapter of the Gospel according to John (cf. Jn 6:69). It ends with the Crucifixion. And in this very way is revealed God's wisdom, which St. Paul was later to explain to us.

Therefore, it is only if we take all things as a journey, step by step, and learn to interpret Scripture in its unity, that we can truly have access to the beauty and richness of Sacred Scripture.

Consequently, one should read everything, but always mindful of the totality of Sacred Scripture, where one part explains the other, one passage on the journey explains the other. On this point, modern exegesis can also be of great help to us.

Let us take, for example, the Book of Isaiah. When the exegetes discovered that from chapter 40 on the author was someone else — Deutero-Isaiah, as he was then called — there was a moment of great panic for Catholic theologians.

Some thought that in this way Isaiah would be destroyed and that at the end, in chapter 53, the vision of the Servant of God was no longer that of Isaiah who lived almost 800 years before Christ. "What shall we do?" people wondered.

We now realize that the whole Book is a process of constantly new interpretations where one enters ever more deeply into the mystery proposed at the beginning, and that what was initially present but still closed, unfolds increasingly. In one book, we can understand the whole journey of Sacred Scripture, which is an ongoing reinterpretation, or rather, a new and better understanding of all that had been said previously.

Step by step, light dawns, and the Christian can grasp what the Lord said to the disciples at Emmaus, explaining to them that it was of him that all the prophets had spoken. The Lord unfolds to us the last rereading; Christ is the key to all things, and only by joining the disciples on the road to Emmaus, only by walking with Christ, by reinterpreting all things in his light, with him, crucified and risen, do we enter into the riches and beauty of Sacred Scripture.

Therefore, I would say that the important point is not to fragment Sacred Scripture. The modern critic himself, as we now see, has enabled us to understand that it is an ongoing journey. And we can also see that it is a journey with a direction and that Christ really is its destination. By starting from Christ, we start the entire journey again and enter into the depths of the Word.

To sum up, I would say that Sacred Scripture must always be read in the light of Christ. Only in this way can we also read and understand Sacred Scripture in our own context today and be truly enlightened by it. We must understand this: Sacred Scripture is a journey with a direction. Those who know the destination can also take all those steps once again now, and can thus acquire a deeper knowledge of the mystery of Christ.

In understanding this, we have also understood the ecclesiality of Sacred Scripture, for these journeys, these steps on the journey, are the steps of a people. It is the People of God who are moving onwards. The true owner of the Word is always the People of God, guided by the Holy Spirit, and inspiration is a complex process: The Holy Spirit leads the people on, the people receive it.

Thus, it is the journey of a people, the People of God. Sacred Scripture should always be interpreted well. But this can happen only if we journey on within this subject, that is, the People of God which lives, is renewed and reconstituted by Christ, but continues to dwell in its own identity.

I would therefore say that there are three interrelated dimensions. The historical dimension, the Christological dimension, and the ecclesiological dimension — of the People on their way — converge. A complete reading is one where all three dimensions are present. Therefore, the Liturgy — the common Liturgy prayed by the People of God — remains the privileged place for understanding the Word; this is partly because it is here that the interpretation becomes prayer and is united with Christ's prayer in the Eucharistic Prayer.

I would like to add here one point that has been stressed by all the Fathers of the Church. I am thinking in particular of a very beautiful text by St. Ephraim and of another by St. Augustine in which he says:

> "If you have understood little, admit it and do not presume that you have understood it all. The Word is always far greater than what you have been able to understand."

And this should be said now, critically, with regard to a certain part of modern exegesis that thinks it has understood everything and that, therefore, after the interpretation it has worked out, there is nothing left to say about it. This is not true. The Word is always greater than the exegesis of the Fathers and critical exegesis because even this comprehends only a part, indeed, a minimal part. The Word is always greater, this is our immense consolation. And on the one hand it is lovely to know that one has only understood a little. It is lovely to know that there is still an inexhaustible treasure and that every new generation will rediscover new treasures and journey on with the greatness of the Word of God that is always before us, guides us, and is ever greater. One should read the Scriptures with an awareness of this.

St. Augustine said: The hare and the donkey drink from the fountain. The donkey drinks more, but each one drinks his fill. Whether we are hares or donkeys, let us be grateful that the Lord enables us to drink from his water.

36. Fr. Gerardo Raul Carcar, a Schönstatt Father who arrived in Rome from Argentina six months ago and today is Vicar Cooperator of the Parish of San Girolamo at Corviale, said that ecclesial movements and new communities are a providential gift for our time. These are entities with a creative impetus, they live the faith and seek new forms of life to find the right place in the Church's mission. Fr. Carcar asked the pope for advice on how he should fit into them to develop a real ministry of unity in the universal Church.

SO I SEE THAT I MUST be briefer. Thank you for your question. I think you mentioned the essential sources of all that we can say about movements. In this sense, your question is also an answer.

I would like to explain immediately that in recent months I have been receiving the Italian bishops on their *ad limina* visits and so have been able to find out a little more about the geography of the faith in Italy. I see many very beautiful things together with the problems that we all know.

I see above all that the faith is still deeply rooted in the Italian heart even if, of course, it is threatened in many ways by today's situations.

The movements also welcome my fatherly role as pastor. Others are more critical and say that movements are out of place. I think, in fact, that situations differ and everything depends on the people in question.

It seems to me that we have two fundamental rules of which you spoke. The first was given to us by St. Paul in his First Letter to the Thessalonians: Do not extinguish charisms. If the Lord gives us new gifts, we must be grateful, even if at times they may be inconvenient. And it is beautiful that without an initiative of the hierarchy but with an initiative from below, as people say, but that also truly comes from on High, that is, as a gift of the Holy Spirit, new forms of life are being born in the Church just as, moreover, they were born down the ages.

At first, they were always inconvenient. Even St. Francis was very inconvenient, and it was very hard for the Pope to give a final canonical form to a reality that by far exceeded legal norms. For St. Francis, it was a very great sacrifice to let himself be lodged in this juridical framework, but in the end this gave rise to a reality that is still alive today and will live on in the future: It gives strength, as well as new elements, to the Church's life.

I wish to say only this: Movements have been born in all the centuries. Even St. Benedict at the outset was a movement. They do not become part of the Church's life without suffering and difficulty. St. Benedict himself had to correct the initial direction that monasticism was taking. Thus, in our century too, the Lord, the Holy Spirit, has given us new initiatives with new aspects of Christian life. Since they are lived by human people with their limitations, they also create difficulties.

So the first rule is: Do not extinguish Christian charisms; be grateful, even if they are inconvenient.

The second rule is: The Church is one; if movements are truly gifts of the Holy Spirit, they belong to and serve the Church and in patient dialogue between pastors and movements, a fruitful form is born where these elements become edifying for the Church today and in the future.

This dialogue is at all levels. Starting with the parish priest, the bishops, and the Successor of Peter, the search for appropriate structures is underway: In many cases it has already borne fruit. In others, we are still studying.

For example, we ask ourselves whether, after five years of experience, it is possible to confirm definitively the Statutes for the Neocatechumenal Way, whether a trial period is necessary, or whether, perhaps, certain elements of this structure need perfecting.

In any case, I knew the Neocatechumens from the very outset. It was a long Way, with many complications that still exist today, but we have found an ecclesial form that has already vastly improved the relationship between the Pastor and the "Way." We are going ahead like this! The same can be said for other movements.

Now, as a synthesis of the two fundamental rules, I would say: gratitude, patience, and also acceptance of the inevitable sufferings. In marriage too, there is always suffering and tension. Yet, the couple goes forward and thus true love matures. The same thing happens in the Church's communities: Let us be patient together.

The different levels of the hierarchy too — from the parish priest, to the bishop, to the Supreme Pontiff — must continually exchange ideas with one another, they must foster dialogue to find together the best road. The experiences of parish priests are fundamental, and so are the experiences of the bishop, and let us say, the universal perspectives of the pope have a theological and pastoral place of their own in the Church.

On the one hand, these different levels of the hierarchy as a whole, and on the other, all life as it is lived in the parish context with patience and openness in obedience to the Lord, really create new vitality in the Church.

Let us be grateful to the Holy Spirit for the gifts he has given to us. Let us be obedient to the voice of the Spirit, but also clear in integrating these elements into our life; lastly, this criterion serves the concrete Church and thus patiently, courageously, and generously, the Lord will certainly guide and help us.

37. Fr. Angelo Mangano, parish priest of San Gelasio, a parish that since 2003 has been entrusted to the pastoral care of the World Church Mission Community, spoke on pastoral work on the Feast of the Chair of St. Peter. He pointed out the importance of developing unity between spiritual life and pastoral life, which is not an organizational technique but coincides with the life of the Church itself. Fr. Mangano asked the Holy Father how to spread the concept of pastoral service among God's People as the true life of the Church, and how to ensure that pastoral work is always nourished by conciliar ecclesiology.

I THINK THERE ARE SEVERAL questions here. One question is: How can we inspire parishes with conciliar ecclesiology and make the faithful live this ecclesiology? Another is how should we behave and make pastoral work spiritual within us?

Let us start with the latter question. There is always a certain tension between what I absolutely have to do and what spiritual reserves I must have. I always see it in St. Augustine, who complains about this in his preaching. I have already cited him: "I long to live with the Word of God from morning to night but I have to be with you." Augustine nonetheless finds this balance by being always available but also by keeping for himself moments of prayer and meditation on the Sacred Word, because otherwise he would no longer be able to say anything.

Here in particular, I would like to underline what you said about the fact that pastoral work must never be mere strategy or administrative work but must always be a spiritual task. Nor, of course, can the latter be totally lacking either, because we are on this earth and such problems exist: the efficient management of money, etc. This too is a sector that cannot be totally ignored.

Nonetheless, the fundamental emphasis must be on the very fact that being a pastor is in itself a spiritual act. You rightly referred to John's Gospel, chapter 10, in which the Lord describes himself as the "Good Shepherd." And as a first definitive moment, Jesus says that the pastor goes first. In other words, it is he who shows the way, he is the first to be an example to others, the first to take the road that is the road for others. The pastor leads the way.

This means that he himself lives first of all on the Word of God; he is a man of prayer, a man of forgiveness, a man who receives and celebrates the sacraments as acts of prayer and encounter with the Lord. He is a man of charity, lived and practiced — thus all the simple acts, conversation, encounter, everything that needs to be done, become spiritual acts in communion with Christ. His *"pro omnibus"* becomes our *"pro meis."* [50]

Then, he goes before us, and I think that in having mentioned this "leading the way," the essential has already been said. Chapter 10 of John continues, saying that Jesus goes before us, giving himself on the Cross. And this is also inevitable for the priest. The offering of himself is also participation in the Cross of Christ, and thanks to this we too can credibly comfort the suffering and be close to the poor, the marginalized, etc.

Therefore, in this program that you have developed, it is fundamental to spiritualize daily pastoral work. It is easier to say this than to do it, but we must try.

Moreover, to be able to spiritualize our work, we must again follow the Lord. The Gospels tell us that by day he worked and by night he was on the mountain with his Father, praying. Here, I must confess my weakness. At night I cannot pray, at night I want to sleep. However, a little free time for the Lord is really necessary: either the celebration of Mass or the prayer of the Liturgy of the Hours and even a brief daily meditation following the Liturgy, the Rosary. But this personal conversation with the Word of God is important; it is only in this way that we can find the reserves to respond to the demands of pastoral life.

---

[50] Literally, "for all" and "for my own." The idea is that the priest deeply internalizes as his very own all that he does as "another Christ" in the service of his people.

The second point: You rightly underlined the ecclesiology of the Council.[51] It seems to me that we must interiorize this ecclesiology far more, that of *Lumen Gentium*[52] and of *Ad Gentes*,[53] which is also an ecclesiological document, as well as the ecclesiology of the minor documents and of *Dei Verbum*.[54]

By interiorizing this vision, we can also attract our people to this vision, which understands that the Church is not merely a large structure, one of these supranational bodies that exist. Although she is a body, the Church is the Body of Christ; hence, she is a spiritual body, as St. Paul said. She is a spiritual reality. I think this is very important: that people see that the Church is not a supranational organization nor an administrative body or power; that she is not a social agency; but indeed that although she does social and supranational work, she is a spiritual body.

I consider that in our prayers with the people, listening with the people to the Word of God, celebrating the sacraments with the People of God, acting with Christ in charity, etc., and especially in our homilies, we should disseminate this vision. It seems to me, in this regard, that the homily affords a marvelous opportunity to be close to the people and to communicate the spirituality taught by the Council. And it thus seems to me that if the homily is developed from prayer, from listening to the Word of God, it is a communication of the content of the Word of God.

The Council truly reaches out to our people, not those fragments in the press that presented an erroneous image of the Council but the true spirituality of the Council. Thus, we must always learn the Word of God anew, with the Council and in

---

[51] The Second Vatican Council.

[52] Dogmatic Constitution on the Church, Second Vatican Council.

[53] Decree on the Mission Activity of the Church, Second Vatican Council

[54] Dogmatic Constitution on the Word of God, Second Vatican Council.

the spirit of the Council, interiorizing its vision. By so doing, we can also communicate with our people and thus truly carry out a task that is both pastoral and spiritual.

⌐⌐

38. Fr. Alberto Pacini, rector of the Basilica of Sant'Anastasia, spoke of perpetual Eucharistic Adoration — especially of the possibility of organizing night vigils — and asked the pope to explain the meaning and value of Eucharistic reparation with reference to sacrilegious thefts and satanic sects.

IN GENERAL WE DO NOT speak much about Eucharistic Adoration, which has truly penetrated our hearts and penetrates the hearts of the people. You have asked this specific question about Eucharistic reparation. This has become a difficult topic.

I remember, when I was young, that on the Feast of the Sacred Heart we prayed using a beautiful prayer by Leo XIII and then one by Pius XI in which reparation had a special place, precisely in reference, already at that time, to sacrilegious acts for which reparation had to be made.

I think we should get to the bottom of it, going back to the Lord himself who offered reparation for the sins of the world, and try to atone for them: Let us say, try to balance the *plus* of evil and the *plus* of goodness. We must not, therefore, leave this great negative *plus* on the scales of the world but must give at least an equal weight to goodness.

This fundamental idea is based on what Christ did. As far as we can understand it, this is the sense of the Eucharistic sacrifice. To counter the great weight of evil that exists in the world and pulls the world downwards, the Lord places another, greater weight, that of the infinite love that enters this world. This is the most important point: God is always the absolute good, but this absolute good actually entered history: Christ makes himself present here and suffers evil to the very end, thereby creating a counterweight of absolute value. Even if we see only empirically the proportions of the *plus* of evil, they are exceeded by the immense *plus* of good, of the suffering of the Son of God.

In this sense there is reparation that is necessary. I think that today it is a little difficult to understand these things. If we see the weight of evil in the world, which is constantly increasing, which seems indisputably to have the upper hand in history, one might — as St. Augustine said in a meditation — truly despair.

But we see that there is an even greater *plus* in the fact that God himself entered history, he made himself share in history and suffered to the very end. This is the meaning of reparation. This *plus* of the Lord is an appeal to us to be on his side, to enter into this great *plus* of love and make it present, even with our weakness. We know that this *plus* was needed for us too, because there is evil in our lives as well. We all survive thanks to the *plus* of the Lord. However, he gives us this gift so that, as the Letter to the Colossians says, we can associate in his abundance and, let us say, effectively increase this abundance during our time in history.

I think that theology ought to do more to enable people to understand this reality of reparation better. In history, there were also some erroneous ideas. In the past few days I have been reading the theological discourses of St. Gregory Nazianzus, who at a certain moment speaks of this aspect and asks:

"For whom did the Lord offer his Blood? The Father did not desire the Blood of the Son, the Father is not cruel, it is not necessary to attribute this to the Father's will, but history wanted it, the needs and imbalances of history desired it; it was necessary to enter into these imbalances and recreate true balance here."

This is very enlightening. But it seems to me that we have not sufficiently mastered the language to make this fact understood to ourselves, and subsequently, also to others. We should not offer to a cruel God the blood of God. But God himself, with his love, must enter into the suffering of history, not only to create a balance, but also a *plus* of love that is stronger than the abundance of the existing evil. This is what the Lord invites us to do.

It seems to me a typically Catholic reality. Luther said: "We cannot add anything." And this is true. And then he said: "Our acts thus do not count for anything." And this is not true, because the Lord's generosity is revealed precisely in his invitation to us to enter and also gives value to our being with him.

We must learn all this better and also be aware of the greatness and generosity of the Lord and the greatness of our vocation. The Lord wants to associate us with his great *plus*. If we begin to understand it, we will be glad that the Lord invites us to do this. It will be a great joy to be taken seriously by the Lord's love.

39. Fr. Francesco Tedeschi, a lecturer at the Pontifical Urban University who also serves at the Basilica of San Bartolomeo on the Tiber Island in Rome, a site that is the memorial of nine twentieth century martyrs, reflected on the exemplarity and capacity for attraction among young people of the figures of the martyrs. The martyrs reveal the beauty of the Christian faith and witness to the world that it is possible to respond to evil with good by basing one's life on the strength of hope. The pope did not choose to add any further words on this reflection.

THE APPLAUSE WE HAVE HEARD shows that you yourself have given ample answers. . . . Therefore, I can only reply to your question: Yes, it is as you have said. And let us meditate upon your words.

～

40. Fr. Krzystzof Wendlik, parochial vicar of Santi Urbano e Lorenzo Parish at Prima Porta, spoke of the problem of relativism in our contemporary culture, and asked the pope for an enlightening word on the relationship between unity of faith and pluralism in theology.

WHAT AN IMPORTANT QUESTION! When I was still a member of the International Theological Commission, we took a year to address this problem. I was the speaker, and I therefore remember it quite well. Yet, I recognize that I am unable to explain the matter in just a few words.

I only wish to say that theology has always been multiple. Let us think of the Fathers in the Middle Ages, the Franciscan School, the Dominican School, then the Late Middle Ages and so on. As we have said, the Word of God is always larger than us. Therefore, we can never come to the end of the outreach of his Word, and various approaches, various types of reflection are necessary.

I would simply like to say: It is important that the theologian, on the one hand, in his responsibility and professional capacity, should seek openings that correspond with the needs and challenges of our time.

On the other hand, he needs to be ever aware that all this is based on the faith of the Church and so he must always refer to the Church's faith. I think if a theologian is personally and profoundly rooted in faith and understands that this work is a reflection on the faith, that he will be able to reconcile unity and plurality.

---

41. The last question was asked by Fr. Luigi Veturi, parish priest of San Giovanni Battista dei Fiorentini. He focused on the theme of sacred art and asked the pope whether this should be better evaluated as a means for communicating faith.

THE ANSWER COULD BE very simple: Yes! I arrived here a little late because I first paid a visit to the Pauline Chapel where restoration work has been underway for several years. I was told that the work will take another two years. I could glimpse between the scaffolding part of this miraculous artwork. And it is worth restoring it well so that it will once again shine out and be a living catechesis.

In saying this, I wanted to recall that Italy is particularly rich in art, and art is a treasure of inexhaustible and incredible catecheses. It is also our duty to know and understand it properly, not in the way that it is sometimes done by art historians, who interpret it only formally in terms of artistic technique.

Rather, we must enter into the content and make the content that inspired this great art live anew. It truly seems to me to be a duty — also in the formation of future priests — to know these treasures and be able to transform all that is present in them and that speaks to us today into a living catechesis.

Thus, the Church also appears as an organism — neither of oppression nor of power, as some people would like to demonstrate — with a unique, spiritually fertile history, one that I would dare to say is not to be found outside the Catholic Church. This is also a sign of the Catholic Church's vitality, which, despite all her weaknesses as well as her sins, has always remained a great spiritual reality, an inspirer that has given us all these riches.

It is therefore our duty to enter into this wealth and to be capable of making ourselves interpreters of this art. May this also be true for pictorial and sculptural art, as well as for sacred music, which is a branch of art that deserves to be revived. I would say that the Gospel variously lived is still today an inspiring force that gives and will give us art.

Above all, the most beautiful sculptures also exist today, which show that the fertility of faith and of the Gospel are not extinguished, that there are still musical compositions today. . . . I believe that it is possible to emphasize a situation that is, let us say, contradictory to art, an even somewhat desperate situation of art.

The Church also inspires today, because faith and the Word of God are inexhaustible. And this gives all of us courage. It gives us the hope that the future world will also have new visions of faith and at the same time, the certainty that the 2,000 years of Christian art that have already passed are still valid and still a "today" of the faith.

VI. Questions Asked by Priests of the Dioceses of Belluno-Feltre and Treviso

The following questions were asked by priests of the Dioceses of Belluno-Feltre and Treviso during an encounter with Pope Benedict XVI at the Church of St. Justin Martyr, Auronzon di Cadore, on July 24, 2007.

≈

42. Your Holiness, I am Fr. Claudio. The question I wanted to ask you is about the formation of conscience, especially in young people, because today it seems more and more difficult to form a consistent conscience, an upright conscience. Good and evil are often confused with having good and bad feelings, the more emotive aspect. So I would like to hear your advice. Thank you.

NOW, TO A CERTAIN EXTENT, this first question reflects a problem of Western culture, since in the last two centuries the concept of "conscience" has undergone a profound transformation. Today, the idea prevails that only what is quantifiable can be rational, which stems from reason. Other things, such as the subjects of religion and morals, should not enter into common reason because they cannot be proven or, rather, put to the "acid test," so to speak.

In this situation, where morals and religion are as it were almost expelled from reason, the subject is the only ultimate criterion of morality and also of religion — the subjective conscience, which knows no other authority. In the end, the subject alone decides, with his feelings and experience, on the possible criteria he has discovered. Yet, in this way the subject becomes an isolated reality and, as you said, the parameters change from one day to the next.

In the Christian tradition, "conscience," *"con-scientia,"* means "with knowledge": That is, ourselves, our being is open and can listen to the voice of being itself, the voice of God. Thus, the voice of the great values is engraved in our being and the greatness of the human being is precisely that he is not closed in on himself; he is not reduced to the material, something quantifiable, but possesses an inner openness to the essentials and has the possibility of listening. In the depths of our being, not only can we listen to the needs of the moment, to material needs, but we can also hear the voice of the Creator himself and thus discern what is good and what is bad.

Of course, this capacity for listening must be taught and encouraged. The commitment to the preaching that we do in church consists of precisely this: Developing this very lofty capacity with which God has endowed human beings for listening to the voice of truth and also the voice of values.

I would say, therefore, that a first step would be to make people aware that our very nature carries in itself a moral message, a divine message that must be deciphered. We can become increasingly better acquainted with it and listen to it if our inner hearing is open and developed.

The actual question now is how to carry out in practice this education in listening, how to make human beings capable of it despite all the forms of modern deafness, how to ensure that this listening, the *Ephphatha*[55] of Baptism, the opening of the inner senses, truly takes place.

In taking stock of the current situation, I would propose the combination of a secular approach and a religious approach,

---

[55] The *Ephphatha* (or *Ephphetha*) is an ancient part of the traditional Rite of Baptism. The priest wet his right thumb with spittle and then touched the ears of the person being baptized saying "*Ephphatha*," that is to say, "Be opened," and then touching the nostrils saying "For a savor of sweetness." In ancient times it was done for converts, catechumens, giving them the right to be initiated into hearing God's word and then being open to the sweetness of grace that comes from being with Christ in the Church. The odd looking Ephphetha is one of the few words in Aramaic (the language Jesus would have spoken on a daily basis) we have preserved in Scripture. In Mark 7:34, Jesus healed a deaf man by touching his ears and tongue with his saliva while saying, "*Ephphatha*."

the approach of faith. Today, we all see that man can destroy the foundations of his existence, his earth; hence, that we can no longer simply do what we like or what seems useful and promising at the time with this earth of ours, with the reality entrusted to us. On the contrary, we must respect the inner laws of creation, of this earth; we must learn these laws and obey these laws if we wish to survive. Consequently, this obedience to the voice of the earth, of being, is more important for our future happiness than the voices of the moment, the desires of the moment.

In short, this is a first criterion to learn: That being itself, our earth, speaks to us and we must listen if we want to survive and to decipher this message of the earth. And if we must be obedient to the voice of the earth, this is even truer for the voice of human life. Not only must we care for the earth, we must respect the other, others: both the other as an individual person, as my neighbor, and others as communities who live in the world and have to live together. And we see that it is only with full respect for this creature of God, this image of God that man is, and with respect for our coexistence on this earth, that we can develop.

And here we reach the point when we need the great moral experiences of humanity. These experiences are born from the encounter with the other, with the community. We need the experience that human freedom is always a shared freedom and can only function if we share our freedom with respect for the values that are common to us all. It seems to me that with these steps it will be possible to make people see the need to obey the voice of being, to respect the dignity of the other, to accept the need to live our respective freedom together as *one* freedom, and through all this to recognize the intrinsic value that can make a dignified communion of life possible among human beings.

Thus, as has been said, we come to the great experiences of humanity in which the voice of being is expressed. We especially come to the experiences of this great historical pilgrimage of the People of God that began with Abraham. In him, not only do we find the fundamental human experiences but also, we can hear through these experiences the voice of the Creator himself, who loves us and has spoken to us. Here, in this context, respecting the human experiences that point out the way to us today and in the future, I believe that the Ten Commandments always have a priority value in which we see the important signposts on our way.

The Ten Commandments reinterpreted, relived in the light of Christ, in the light of the life of the Church and of her experiences, point to certain fundamental and essential values. Together, the Fourth and Sixth Commandments suggest the importance of our body, of respecting the laws of the body and of sexuality and love, the value of faithful love, of the family; the Fifth Commandment points to the value of life and also the value of community life; the Seventh Commandment regards the value of sharing the earth's goods and of a fair distribution of these goods and of the stewardship of God's creation; the Eighth Commandment points to the great value of truth. If, therefore, in the Fourth, Fifth and Sixth Commandments we have love of neighbor, in the Seventh we have the truth.

None of this works without communion with God, without respect for God and God's presence in the world. In any case, a world without God becomes an arbitrary and egoistic world. There is light and hope only if God appears. Our life has a meaning that we must not produce ourselves but which precedes us and guides us. In this sense, therefore, I would say that together, we should take the obvious routes that today even the lay conscience can easily discern. We should therefore seek to guide people to the deepest voices, to the true voice of the conscience that is communicated through the great tradition of prayer, of the moral life of the Church. Thus, in a process of patient education, I think we can all learn to live and to find true life.

43. I am Fr. Mauro, Your Holiness. In exercising our pastoral ministry, we are increasingly burdened by many duties. Our tasks in the management and administration of parishes, pastoral organization and assistance to people in difficulty are piling up. I ask you, what are the priorities we should aim for in our ministry as priests and parish priests to avoid fragmentation on the one hand and on the other, dispersion? Thank you.

THAT IS A VERY REALISTIC question, is it not? I am also somewhat familiar with this problem, with all the daily procedures, with all the necessary audiences, with all that there is to do. Yet, it is necessary to determine the right priorities and not to forget the essential: the proclamation of the Kingdom of God.

On hearing your question, I remembered the Gospel of the mission of the 70 disciples. For this first important mission that Jesus had them undertake, the Lord gave them three orders that on the whole I think express the great priorities in the work of a disciple of Christ, a priest, in our day too. The three imperatives are: to pray, to provide care, to preach.

I think we should find the balance between these three basic imperatives and keep them ever present as the heart of our work. Prayer: Which is to say, without a personal relationship with God, nothing else can function, for we cannot truly bring God, the divine reality or true human life to people unless we ourselves live them in a deep, true relationship of friendship with God in Jesus Christ.

Hence, the daily celebration of the Holy Eucharist is a fundamental encounter where the Lord speaks to me and I speak to the Lord who gives himself through my hands. Without the prayer of the Hours, in which we join in the great prayer of the entire People of God beginning with the Psalms of the ancient people who are renewed in the faith of the Church, and without personal prayer, we cannot be good priests for we would lose the essence of our ministry. The first imperative is to be a man of God, in the sense of a man in friendship with Christ and with his saints.

Then comes the second command. Jesus said: Tend the sick, seek those who have strayed, those who are in need. This is the Church's love for the marginalized and the suffering. Rich people can also be inwardly marginalized and suffering. "To take care of" refers to all human needs, which are always profoundly oriented to God. Thus, as has been said, it is necessary for us to know our sheep, to be on good terms with the people entrusted to us, to have human contact, and not to lose our humanity, because God was made man and consequently strengthened all dimensions of our being as humans.

However, as I said, the human and the divine always go hand in hand. To my mind, the sacramental ministry is also part of this "tending" in its multiple forms. The ministry of Reconciliation is an act of extraordinary caring that the person needs in order to be perfectly healthy. Thus, this sacramental care begins with Baptism, which is the fundamental renewal of our life, and extends to the Sacrament of Reconciliation and the Anointing of the Sick. Of course, all the other sacraments and also the Eucharist involve great care for souls.

We have to care for people but above all — this is our mandate — for their souls. We must think of the many illnesses and moral and spiritual needs that exist today and that we must face, guiding people to the encounter with Christ in the sacrament, helping them to discover prayer and meditation, being silently recollected in church with this presence of God. And then, preaching.

What do we preach? We proclaim the Kingdom of God. But the Kingdom of God is not a distant utopia in a better world that may be achieved in 50 years' time, or who knows when. The Kingdom of God is God himself, God close to us who became very close in Christ. This is the Kingdom of God: God himself is near to us and we must draw close to this God who is close for he was made man, remains man, and is always with us in his Word, in the Most Holy Eucharist, and in all believers.

Therefore, proclaiming the Kingdom of God means speaking of God today, making present God's words, the Gospel that is God's presence and, of course, making present the God who made himself present in the Holy Eucharist. By interweaving these three priorities and, naturally, taking into account all the human aspects, including our own limitations that we must recognize, we can properly fulfill our priesthood. This humility that recognizes the limitations of our own strength is important as well. All that we cannot do, the Lord must do. And there is also the ability to delegate and to collaborate. All this must always go with the fundamental imperatives of praying, tending, and preaching.

44. My name is Fr. Daniele. Your Holiness, the Veneto is an area with a steady influx of immigrants where a sizable number of non-Christians are present. This situation confronts our dioceses with a new, internal task of evangelization. Moreover, this represents a certain difficulty since we have to reconcile the needs of Gospel proclamation with those of a respectful dialogue with other religions. What pastoral instructions can you suggest? Thank you.

YOU ARE NATURALLY IN CLOSE touch with this situation. And in this regard, I may be unable to give you much practical advice, but I can say that in all the *ad limina* visits, whether the bishops come from Asia, Africa, Latin America, or every part of Italy, I am always confronted with such situations.

A uniform world no longer exists. All the other continents, the other religions, the other ways of living human life are present especially in the West. We are living a permanent encounter where we resemble the ancient Church because she experienced the same situation. Christians formed a tiny minority, a mustard seed that began to sprout, surrounded by very different religions and ways of life.

We must learn once again, therefore, all that the first generations of Christians experienced. In his First Letter, St. Peter said: "Always be prepared to make a defense to any one who calls you to account for the hope that is in you" (1 Pet. 3:15).

Thus, he formulated for the ordinary person of that time, for the ordinary Christian, the need to combine proclamation and dialogue.

He did not say formally: "Proclaim the Gospel to everyone." He said: "You must be able, ready, to account for the hope that is in you." I think that this is the necessary synthesis between dialogue and proclamation.

The first point is that the reason for our hope must be ever present within us. We must be people who live faith and think faith, people with an inner knowledge of it. So it is that faith becomes reason within us, it becomes reasonable. Meditation on the Gospel and in this case, proclamation, the homily, and catechesis to enable people to ponder faith, already constitute fundamental elements in this web of dialogue and proclamation. We ourselves must think faith, live faith, and, as priests, find different ways to make faith present so that our Christian Catholics can find the conviction, readiness, and ability to account for their faith.

This proclamation that transmits the faith to today's conscience must have many forms. The homily and catechesis are indisputably two of its principal forms, but there are also many ways of meeting, such as seminars on faith, lay movements, etc., where people talk about faith and learn the faith. All this makes us capable, first of all, of truly living as the neighbors of non-Catholics — here, mainly Orthodox Christians, Protestants, and also exponents of other religions, Muslims and others.

The first aspect is to live beside them, recognizing with them their neighbor, our neighbor; thus, living love of neighbor on the front line as an expression of our faith. I think that this is already a very powerful witness and also a form of proclamation:

Truly living love of neighbor with these others, recognizing the latter, recognizing them as our neighbor so that they can see: This "love of neighbor" is for me. If this happens, we will be able to more easily present the source of our behavior — in other words, that love of neighbor is an expression of our faith.

Thus, our dialogue cannot move on suddenly to the great mysteries of faith, although Muslims have a certain knowledge of Christ that denies his divinity but at least recognizes him as a great prophet. They love Our Lady. These are consequently elements that we have in common, even in faith, and are starting points for dialogue.

A perception of fundamental understanding on the values we should live is practical, feasible, and above all necessary. Here too, we have a treasure in common because Muslims come from the religion of Abraham, reinterpreted and relived in ways to be studied and to which we should finally respond. Yet, the great substantial experience of the Ten Commandments is present, and this seems to me a point that requires further investigation. Moving on to the great mysteries seems to me to be moving to a level that is far from easy and impossible to attain at large meetings. Perhaps the seed should enter hearts, so that here and there the response of faith in a more specific dialogue may mature. But what we can and must do is to seek a consensus on the fundamental values expressed in the Ten Commandments, summed up in love of neighbor and love of God, and which can thus be interpreted in the various life contexts.

We are at least on a common journey towards the God of Abraham, Isaac, and Jacob, the God who is ultimately the God with the human face, the God present in Jesus Christ. But if the latter step is to be made in intimate, personal encounters or small groups, the journey towards this God, from which derives these values that make life in common possible, I think this is feasible also at larger meetings. As a result, in my opinion a humble, patient form of proclamation should be undertaken here, which awaits but already realizes our life in accordance with knowledge enlightened by God.

⌇

45. I am Fr. Samuele. We have accepted your invitation to pray, care for people, and preach. We are taking you seriously by caring for you yourself; so, to express our affection, we have brought you several bottles of wholesome wine from our region, which we will make sure that you receive through our bishop. So now for my question. We are seeing an enormous increase in situations of divorced people who remarry, live together, and ask priests to help them with their spiritual life. These people often come to us with a heartfelt plea for access to the sacraments. These realities need to be faced, and the sufferings they cause must be shared. Holy Father, may I ask you what are the human, spiritual, and pastoral approaches with which one can combine compassion and truth? Thank you.

YES, THIS IS INDEED A painful problem, and there is certainly no simple solution to resolve it. This problem makes us all suffer because we all have people close to us who are in this situation. We know it causes them sorrow and pain because they long to be in full communion with the Church. The previous bond of matrimony reduces their participation in the life of the Church.

What can be done? I would say: As far as possible, we would naturally put prevention first. Hence, preparation for marriage becomes ever more fundamental and necessary. Canon Law presupposes that man as such, even without much education, intends to contract a marriage in harmony with human nature, as mentioned in the first chapters of Genesis. He is a human being, his nature is human, and consequently he knows what marriage is. He intends to behave as human nature dictates to him. Canon Law starts from this presupposition. It is something compulsory: Man is man, nature is what it is and tells him this.

Today, however, this axiom, which holds that man prompted by his nature will make one faithful marriage, has been transformed into a somewhat different axiom. *"Volunt contrahere matrimonium sicut ceteri hominess."*[56] It is no longer nature alone that speaks, but the *"ceteri homines"*: What everyone does. And what everyone does today is not simply to enter into natural marriage, in accordance with the Creator, in accordance with creation. What the *"ceteri homines"* do is marry with the idea that one day their marriage might fail and that they will then be able to move on to another one, to a third or even a fourth marriage.

This model of what "everyone does" thus becomes one that is contrary to what nature says. In this way, it becomes normal to marry, divorce, and remarry, and no one thinks this is something contrary to human nature, or in any case those who do are few and far between. Therefore, to help people achieve a real marriage, not only in the sense of the Church but also of the

---

[56] "They desire to contract marriage just as other men do." The sense here is that although it is of God's design that man and woman be one flesh, which is marriage, today more and more prevailing fads or bad practices influence people to divorce and remarry or live outside of wedlock or be promiscuous, etc. This is today justified on the grounds that "Everybody does those things, so why shouldn't I?"

Creator, we must revive their capacity for listening to nature. Let us return to the first query, the first question: rediscovering within what everyone does, what nature itself tells us, which is so different from what this modern custom dictates. Indeed, it invites us to marry for life, with lifelong fidelity including the suffering that comes from growing together in love.

Thus, these preparatory courses for marriage must be a rectification of the voice of nature, of the Creator, within us, a rediscovery, beyond what all the *"ceteri homines"* do, of what our own being intimately tells us. In this situation, therefore, distinguishing between what everyone else does and what our being tells us, these preparatory courses for marriage must be a journey of rediscovery. They must help us learn anew what our being tells us. They must help couples reach the true decision of marriage in accordance with the Creator and the Redeemer. Hence, these preparatory courses are of great importance in order to "learn oneself," to learn the true intention for marriage.

But preparation is not enough; the great crises come later. Consequently, ongoing guidance, at least in the first ten years, is of the utmost importance. In the parish, therefore, it is not only necessary to provide preparatory courses but also communion in the journey that follows, guidance, and mutual help. May priests, but not on their own, and families, which have already undergone such experiences and are familiar with such suffering and temptations, be available in moments of crisis. The presence of a network of families that help one another is important, and different movements can make a considerable contribution.

The first part of my answer provides for prevention, not only in the sense of preparation but also of guidance and for the presence of a network of families to assist in this contemporary situation where everything goes against faithfulness for life. It is necessary to help people find this faithfulness and learn it, even in the midst of suffering. However, in the case of failure, in other words, when the spouses are incapable of adhering to their original intention, there is always the question of whether it was a real decision in the sense of the sacrament.

As a result, one possibility is the process for the declaration of nullity. If their marriage were authentic, which would prevent them from remarrying, the Church's permanent presence would help these people to bear the additional suffering. In the first case, we have the suffering that goes with overcoming this crisis and learning a hard-fought for and mature fidelity. In the second case, we have the suffering of being in a new bond that is not sacramental, hence, does not permit full communion in the sacraments of the Church. Here it would be necessary to teach and to learn how to live with this suffering. We return to this point, to the first question of the other diocese.

In our generation, in our culture, we have to rediscover the value of suffering in general, and we have to learn that suffering can be a very positive reality that helps us to mature, to become more ourselves, and to be closer to the Lord who suffered for us and suffers with us. Even in the latter situation, therefore, the presence of the priest, families, movements, personal and communitarian communion in these situations, the helpful love of one's neighbor, a very specific love, is of the greatest importance. And I think that only this love, felt by the Church and expressed in the solidarity of many, can help these people recognize that they are loved by Christ and are members of the Church despite their difficult situation. Thus, it can help them to live the faith.

46. My name is Fr. Saverio, so of course my question concerns the missions. This year is the 50th anniversary of the encyclical Fidei Donum. *Many priests in our diocese, myself included, have accepted the Pope's invitation; they, we, have lived and are living the experience of the mission ad gentes.*[57] *There can be no doubt that this is an extraordinary experience, which in my modest opinion could be shared by a great number of priests with a view to exchanges between sister churches. Since the instruction in the encyclical is still timely today, given the dwindling number of priests in our countries, how and with what attitude should it be accepted and lived both by the priests who are sent out and by the whole diocese? Thank you.*

THANK YOU. I WOULD FIRST like to thank all these *fidei donum* priests and the dioceses. As I have already mentioned, I have received a great number of *ad limina* visits from bishops of Asia, Africa, and Latin America, and they all tell me: "We are badly in need of *fidei donum* priests, and we are deeply grateful for the work they do. They make present, often in extremely difficult situations, the catholicity of the Church, and they make visible the great universal communion that we form, as well as the love for our distant neighbor who becomes close in the situation of the *fidei donum* priest."

---

[57] "Mission to the peoples," refers to the Church efforts to evangelize all peoples according to Christ's command before his Ascension (cf. Matthew 28:19). "*Fidei donum priests*" ("gift of faith") describes priests who are "loaned" from one part of the world to another region where priestly vocations are lacking. In 1957, Pope Pius XII in his encyclical *Fidei Donum* asked that European dioceses send priests to help in Africa. In 1960 Bl. Pope John XXIII did something similar for Latin America. The idea is that bishops and priests are ordained for and serve the whole Church, not just a little geographically circumscribed area.

In the past 50 years I have almost tangibly felt and seen this great gift, truly given, in my conversations with priests who say to us: "Do not think that we Africans are now quite self-sufficient; we are still in need of the visibility of the great communion of the universal Church." I would say that we all need to be visible as Catholics and we need to love the neighbor who comes from afar and thus finds his neighbor.

Today, the situation has changed in the sense that we in Europe also receive priests from Africa, Latin America, and even from other parts of Europe. This enables us to perceive the beauty of this exchange of gifts, this gift of one to the other, because we all need one another: It is precisely in this way that the Body of Christ grows.

To sum up, I would like to say that this gift was and is a great gift, perceived in the Church as such: In so many situations that I cannot describe here, which involve social problems, problems of development, problems of the proclamation of the faith, problems of loneliness, the need for the presence of others, these priests are a gift in which the dioceses and particular churches recognize the presence of Christ who gives himself for us.

At the same time, they recognize that Eucharistic Communion is not only a supranatural communion but becomes concrete communion in this gift of self of diocesan priests who make themselves available to other dioceses, and that the network of particular churches thus truly becomes a network of love.

Thanks to all those who have made this gift. I can only encourage bishops and priests to continue making this gift. I know that today, with the shortage of vocations, it is becoming more and more difficult in Europe to make this gift; but we already have the experience that other continents in turn, such as especially India and Africa, also give us priests. Reciprocity continues to be of paramount importance. Precisely the experience that we are the Church sent out into the world that everyone knows and loves, is very necessary and also constitutes the power of proclamation.

Thus, people can see that the mustard seed bears fruit and ceaselessly, time and again, becomes a great tree in which the birds of the air find repose. Thank you and be strong.

47. Fr. Alberto: Holy Father, young people are our future and our hope: But they sometimes see life as a difficulty rather than an opportunity; not as a gift for themselves and for others but as something to be consumed on the spot; not as a future to be built but as aimless wandering. The contemporary mind-set demands that young people be happy and perfect all of the time. The result is that every tiny failure and the least difficulty are no longer seen as causes for growth but as a defeat. All this often leads to irreversible acts such as suicide, which wound the hearts of those who love them and of society as a whole. What can you tell us educators who feel all too often that our hands are tied and that we have no answers? Thank you.

I THINK YOU HAVE JUST given us a precise description of a life in which God does not figure. At first sight, it seems as if we do not need God or indeed, that without God we would be freer and the world would be grander. But after a certain time, we see in our young people what happens when God disappears. As

Nietzsche said: "The great light has been extinguished, the sun has been put out." Life is then a chance event. It becomes a thing that I must seek to do the best I can with and use life as though it were a thing that serves my own immediate, tangible, and achievable happiness.

But the big problem is that were God not to exist and were he not also the Creator of my life, life would actually be a mere cog in evolution, nothing more; it would have no meaning in itself. Instead, I must seek to give meaning to this component of being.

Currently, I see in Germany, but also in the United States, a somewhat fierce debate raging between so-called "creationism" and evolutionism, presented as though they were mutually exclusive alternatives: Those who believe in the Creator would not be able to conceive of evolution, and those who instead support evolution would have to exclude God. This antithesis is absurd because, on the one hand, there are so many scientific proofs in favor of evolution, which appears to be a reality we can see and which enriches our knowledge of life and being as such. But on the other, the doctrine of evolution does not answer every query, especially the great philosophical question: Where does everything come from? And how did everything start, which ultimately led to man?

I believe this is of the utmost importance. This is what I wanted to say in my lecture at Regensburg: That reason should be more open, that it should indeed perceive these facts but also realize that they are not enough to explain all of reality. They are insufficient. Our reason is broader and can also see that our reason is not basically something irrational, a product of irrationality, but that reason, creative reason, precedes everything and we are truly the reflection of creative reason. We were thought of and desired; thus, there is an idea that preceded me, a feeling that preceded me that I must discover, that I must follow, because it will at last give meaning to my life. This seems to me to be the first point: To discover that my being is truly reasonable, it was thought of, it has meaning. And my important mission is to discover this meaning, to live it, and thereby contribute a new element to the great cosmic harmony conceived of by the Creator.

If this is true, then difficulties also become moments of growth, of the process and progress of my very being, which has meaning from conception until the very last moment of life. We can get to know this reality of meaning that precedes all of us, we can also rediscover the meaning of pain and suffering; there is of course one form of suffering that we must avoid and must distance from the world: All the pointless suffering caused by dictatorships and erroneous systems, by hatred, and by violence. However, in suffering there is also a profound meaning, and only if we can give meaning to pain and suffering can our life mature.

I would say, above all, that there can be no love without suffering, because love always implies renouncement of myself, letting myself go and accepting the other in his otherness; it implies a gift of myself and therefore, emerging from myself. All this is pain and suffering, but precisely in this suffering caused by the losing of myself for the sake of the other, for the loved one and hence, for God, I become great, and my life finds love, and in love finds its meaning. The inseparability of love and suffering, of love and God, are elements that must enter into the modern conscience to help us live.

In this regard, I would say that it is important to help the young discover God, to help them discover the true love that precisely in renunciation becomes great and so also enables them to discover the inner benefit of suffering, which makes me freer and greater. Of course, to help young people find these elements, companionship and guidance are always essential, whether through the parish, Catholic Action, or a movement. It is only in the company of others that we can also reveal this great dimension of our being to the new generations.

⸻

48. I am Fr. Francesco. Holy Father, one sentence you wrote in your book made a deep impression on me: "[But] what did Jesus actually bring if not world peace, universal prosperity and a better world? What has he brought? The answer is very simple: 'God. He has brought God'" (Jesus of Nazareth, English edition, p. 44); *I find the clarity and truth of this citation disarming. This is my question: There is talk about the new evangelization, the new proclamation of the Gospel — this was also the main theme of the Synod of our diocese, Belluno-Feltre — but what should we do so that this God, the one treasure brought by Jesus and who all too often appears hazy to many, shines forth anew in our homes and becomes the water that quenches even the thirst of the many who seem no longer to be thirsting? Thank you.*

THANK YOU. YOURS IS A fundamental question. The fundamental question of our pastoral work is how to bring God to the world, to our contemporaries. Of course, bringing God is a multidimensional task: Already in Jesus' preaching, in his life and his death we see how this One develops in so many dimensions. I think that we should always be mindful of two things: On the one hand, the Christian proclamation.

Christianity is not a highly complicated collection of so many dogmas that it is impossible for anyone to know them all; it is not something exclusively for academicians who can study these things, but it is something simple: God exists, and God is close in Jesus Christ.

Thus, to sum up, Jesus Christ himself said that the Kingdom of God had arrived. Basically, what we preach is one, simple thing. All the dimensions subsequently revealed are dimensions of this one thing, and all people do not have to know everything but must certainly enter into the depths and into the essential. In this way, the different dimensions also unfold with ever-increasing joy. But in practice what should be done?

I think, speaking of pastoral work today, that we have already touched on the essential points. But to continue in this direction, bringing God implies above all, on the one hand, love, and on the other, hope and faith. Thus, the dimension of life lived, bearing the best witness for Christ, the best proclamation, is always the life of true Christians.

If we see that families nourished by faith live in joy, that they also experience suffering in profound and fundamental joy, that they help others, loving God and their neighbor, in my opinion this is the most beautiful proclamation today. For me too, the most comforting proclamation is always that of seeing Catholic families or personalities who are penetrated by faith: The presence of God truly shines out in them, and they bring the "living water" that you mentioned.

The fundamental proclamation is, therefore, precisely that of the actual life of Christians. Of course, there is also the proclamation of the Word. We must spare no effort to ensure that the Word is listened to and known. Today, there are numerous schools of the Word and of the conversation with God in Sacred Scripture, a conversation that necessarily also becomes prayer, because the purely theoretical study of Sacred Scripture is a form of listening that is merely intellectual and would not be a real or satisfactory encounter with the Word of God.

If it is true that in Scripture and in the Word of God it is the Living Lord God who speaks to us, who elicits our response and our prayers, then schools of Scripture must also be schools of prayer, of dialogue with God, of drawing intimately close to God: consequently, the whole proclamation.

Then, of course, I would say the sacraments.

All the saints also always come with God. It is important — Sacred Scripture tell us from the very outset — that God never comes by himself but comes accompanied and surrounded by the angels and saints.

In the great stained glass window in St. Peter's which portrays the Holy Spirit, what I like so much is the fact that God is surrounded by a throng of angels and living beings who are an expression, an emanation, so to speak, of God's love. And with God, with Christ, with the man who is God and with God who is man, Our Lady arrives.

This is very important. God, the Lord, has a mother and in his mother we truly recognize God's motherly goodness. Our Lady, Mother of God, is the Help of Christians, she is our permanent comfort, our great help. I see this, too, in the dialogue with the bishops of the world, of Africa and lately also of Latin America; I see that love for Our Lady is the driving force of catholicity. In Our Lady we recognize all God's tenderness; so, fostering and living out Our Lady's, Mary's, joyful love is a very great gift of catholicity.

Then there are the saints. Every place has its own saint. This is good because in this way we see the range of colors of God's one light and of his love that comes close to us. It means discovering the saints in their beauty, in their drawing close to me in the Word, so that in a specific saint I may find expressed precisely for me the inexhaustible Word of God, and then all the aspects of parochial life, even the human ones. We must not always be in the clouds, in the loftiest clouds of mystery. We must have our feet firmly planted on the ground and together live the joy of being a great family: the great little family of the parish; the great family of the diocese, the great family of the universal Church.

In Rome I can see all this, I can see how people from every part of the world who do not know one another are actually acquainted because they all belong to the family of God. They are close to one another because they all possess the love of the Lord, the love of Our Lady, the love of the saints, Apostolic Succession, and the Successor of Peter and the bishops.

I would say that this joy of catholicity with its many different hues is also the joy of beauty. We have here the beauty of a beautiful organ; the beauty of a very beautiful church, the beauty that has developed in the Church. I think this is a marvelous testimony of God's presence and of the truth of God. Truth is expressed in beauty, and we must be grateful for this beauty and seek to do our utmost to ensure that it is ever present, that it develops and continues to grow. In this way, I believe that God will be very concretely in our midst.

49. I am Fr. Lorenzo, a parish priest. Holy Father, the faithful expect only one thing from priests: that they be experts in encouraging the encounter of human beings with God. These are not my own words but something Your Holiness said in an address to the clergy. My spiritual director at the seminary, in those trying sessions of spiritual direction, said to me: "Lorenzino, humanly we've made it, but. . . ," and when he said "but," what he meant was that I preferred playing football[58] to Eucharistic Adoration. And he meant that this did my vocation no good and that it was not right to dispute lessons of morals and law, because the teachers knew more about them than I did. And with that "but," who knows what else he meant. I now think of him in heaven, and in any case I say some requiems for him. In spite of everything, I have been a priest for thirty-four years and I am happy about that, too. I have worked no miracles nor have I known any disasters or perhaps I did not recognize them. I feel that "humanly we've made it" is a great compliment. However, does not bringing man close to God and God to man pass above all through what we call humanity, which is indispensable even for us priests?

THANK YOU. I WOULD SIMPLY say "yes" to what you said at the end. Catholicism, somewhat simplistically, has always been considered the religion of the great *"et ... et"*[59]: not of great forms of

---

[58] Soccer.

[59] *"Et ... et"* is a common Latin construction meaning "both ... and." The Pope is saying that this is not an "either ... or" concept, by which one thing excludes another. Instead, it is inclusive.

exclusivism but of synthesis. The exact meaning of "Catholic" is "synthesis." I would therefore be against having to choose between either playing football or studying Sacred Scripture or Canon Law. Let us do both these things.

It is great to do sports. I am not a great sportsman, yet I used to like going to the mountains when I was younger; now I only go on some very easy excursions, but I always find it very beautiful to walk here in this wonderful earth that the Lord has given to us. Therefore, we cannot always live in exalted meditation; perhaps a saint on the last step of his earthly pilgrimage could reach this point, but we normally live with our feet on the ground and our eyes turned to heaven.

Both these things are given to us by the Lord and therefore loving human things, loving the beauties of this earth, is not only very human but also very Christian and truly Catholic. I would say — and it seems to me that I have already mentioned this earlier — that this aspect is also part of a good and truly Catholic pastoral care: Living in the *"et ... et";* living the humanity and humanism of the human being, all the gifts that the Lord has lavished upon us and that we have developed; and at the same time, not forgetting God, because ultimately, the great light comes from God and then it is only from him that comes the light that gives joy to all these aspects of the things that exist.

Therefore, I would simply like to commit myself to the great Catholic synthesis, to this *"et ... et";* to be truly human. And each person, in accordance with his or her own gifts and charism, should not only love the earth and the beautiful things the Lord has given us, but also be grateful because God's light shines on earth and bathes everything in splendor and beauty.

In this regard, let us live catholicity joyfully. This would be my answer. *(Applause)*

⌁

50. I am Fr. Arnaldo. Holy Father, pastoral and ministerial requirements in addition to the reduced number of priests impel our Bishops to review the distribution of clergy, resulting in an accumulation of tasks for one priest as well as responsibility for more than one parish. This closely affects many communities of the baptized and requires that we priests — priests and lay people — live and exercise the pastoral ministry together. How is it possible to live this change in pastoral organization, giving priority to the spirituality of the Good Shepherd? Thank you, Your Holiness.

YES, LET US RETURN TO this question of pastoral priorities and how to be a parish priest today. A little while ago, a French bishop who was a religious and so had never been a parish priest, said to me: "Your Holiness, I would like you to explain to me what a parish priest is. In France we have these large pastoral units covering five, six, or seven parishes, and the parish priest becomes a coordinator of bodies, of different initiatives." But it seemed to him, since he was so busy coordinating the different bodies he was obliged to deal with, that he no longer had the possibility of a personal encounter with his sheep. Since he was a bishop, hence, the pastor of a large parish, he wondered if this system were right or whether we ought to rediscover a possibility for the parish priest to be truly a parish priest, hence, pastor of his flock.

I could not, of course, come up with the recipe for an instant solution to the situation in France, but the problem in general is: to ensure that, despite the new situations and new forms of responsibility, the parish priest does not forfeit his closeness to the people, his truly being in person the shepherd of this flock entrusted to him by the Lord. Situations are not the same: I am thinking of the bishops in their dioceses with widely differing situations; they must see clearly how to ensure that the parish priest continues to be a pastor and does not become a holy bureaucrat.

In any case, I think that a first opportunity in which we can be present for the people entrusted to us is precisely the sacramental life. In the Eucharist we are together and can and must meet one another; the Sacrament of Penance and Reconciliation is a very personal encounter; Baptism is a personal encounter and not only the moment of the conferral of the Sacrament. I would say that all these sacraments have a context of their own: Baptizing entails offering the young family a little catechesis, speaking to them so that Baptism may also become a personal encounter and an opportunity for a very concrete catechesis.

Preparation for First Communion, Confirmation, and Marriage is likewise always an opportunity for the parish priest, the priest, to meet people personally; he is the preacher and administrator of the sacraments in a way that always involves the human dimension. A sacrament is never merely a ritual act, but the ritual and sacramental act strengthens the human context in which the priest or parish priest acts.

Furthermore, I think it very important to find the right ways to delegate. It is not right that the parish priest should only coordinate other bodies. Rather, he should delegate in various ways, and obviously at Synods — and here in this diocese you have had the Synod — a way is found to free the parish priest sufficiently. This should be done in such a way that on the one hand he retains responsibility for the totality of pastoral units entrusted to him. He should not be reduced to being mainly and above all a coordinating bureaucrat. On the contrary, he should be the one who holds the essential reins himself but can also rely on collaborators.

I believe that this is one of the important and positive results of the Council: the co-responsibility of the entire parish, for the parish priest is no longer the only one to animate everything. Since we all form a parish together, we must all collaborate and help so that the parish priest is not left on his own, mainly as a coordinator, but truly discovers that he is a pastor who is backed up in these common tasks in which, together, the parish lives and is fulfilled.

Thus, I would say that, on the one hand, this coordination and vital responsibility for the whole parish, and on the other, the sacramental life and preaching as a center of parish life, could also today, in circumstances that are of course more difficult, make it possible to be a parish priest who may not know each person by name, as the Lord says of the Good Shepherd, but one who really knows his sheep and is really their pastor who calls and guides them.

51. I am asking the last question and I am very tempted to keep quiet for it is a small question, Your Holiness, and after you have

nine times found the way to speak to us of God and so exalt us, I
feel that what I am about to ask you is trivial and poor, as it were;
yet I shall do so! Just a word for those of my generation who
trained during the years of the Council and set out with enthusi-
asm and perhaps also the ambition to change the world. We
worked very hard, and today we are in a somewhat tricky position
because we are worn out, many of our dreams failed to come true,
and we feel somewhat lonely. The oldest say to us, "You see, we
were right to have been more prudent"; and the younger ones
sometimes taunt us for being "nostalgic for the Council." This is
our question: Can we still bring a gift to our Church, especially
with that attachment to people that we feel has marked us? Please
help us to recover our hope and serenity.

THANK YOU. THIS IS AN important question with which I am
well acquainted. I also lived at the time of the Council. I was
in St. Peter's Basilica with great enthusiasm and saw new doors
opening. It really seemed to be the new Pentecost in which
the Church could once again convince humanity, after the
world had distanced itself from the Church in the eighteenth
and nineteenth centuries; it seemed that the Church and the
world were meeting again and that a Christian world and a
Church of the world, truly open to the world, were being born
anew. We had so many hopes but in fact things turned out to
be more difficult.

However, the great legacy of the Council that opened up a
new road endures; it is still a *magna carta*[60] of the Church's journey, very essential and fundamental. Why did this happen?

---

[60] "Great charter."

Perhaps I would like to begin with a historical observa-
tion. A postconciliar period is almost always very difficult.
The important Council of Nicaea — which for us really is
the foundation of our faith, in fact, we confess the faith formulated at Nicaea — did not lead to a situation of reconciliation and unity as Constantine, who organized this great
Council, had hoped. It was followed instead by a truly chaotic
situation of in-fighting.

In his book on the Holy Spirit, St. Basil compares the situation of the Church subsequent to the Council of Nicea to a
naval battle at night in which no one recognizes the other but
everyone fights everyone else. It really was a situation of total
chaos: Thus, St. Basil painted in strong colors the drama of the
postconciliar period, the aftermath of Nicaea.

Fifty years later, for the First Council of Constantinople,
the Emperor invited St. Gregory of Nazianzus to take part in the
Council. St. Gregory answered: "No. I will not come because I
know these things, I know that all Councils produce nothing
but confusion and fighting so I shall not be coming." And he
did not go.

Thus, in retrospect, today is not as great a surprise as it
would have been at the outset for us all to digest the Council,
its important message. To integrate it in the Church's life, to
accept it so that it may become the life of the Church, to
assimilate it in the various milieus of the Church, means suffering. And it is only in suffering that growth is achieved.
Growing always brings suffering because it means emerging
from one stage and moving on to the next; and we must note
that in the concrete postconciliar period, there are two great
historical caesurae.

In the postconciliar period, we had the pause in 1968, the beginning or "explosion" — I would dare to call it — of the great cultural crisis of the West. The postwar generation had come to an end. This was the generation that, after all the destruction and seeing the horrors of war and fighting and noting the tragedy of the great ideologies that truly led people to the brink of war, rediscovered the Christian roots of Europe. And we had begun to rebuild Europe with these lofty inspirations. However, once this generation had disappeared, all the failures, the shortcomings in this reconstruction, and the widespread poverty in the world became visible. Thus, the crisis in Western culture, I would call it a cultural revolution that wanted radical change, burst out. It was saying: In 2,000 years of Christianity, we have not created a better world. We must start again from zero in an entirely new way. Marxism seems to be the scientific recipe for creating a new world at last. And in this — we said — serious clash between the new and healthy modernity desired by the Council and the crisis of modernity, everything becomes difficult, just as it was after the First Council of Nicaea.

Some were of the opinion that this cultural revolution was what the Council desired. They identified this new Marxist cultural revolution with the Council's intentions. This faction said: "This is the Council. Literally, the texts are still somewhat antiquated, but this is the spirit behind the written words, this is the will of the Council, this is what we have to do."

On the other hand, however, was a reaction that said: "This is the way to destroy the Church." This reaction — let us say — was utterly opposed to the Council, the anticonciliar approach and — let us say — the timid, humble effort to achieve the true spirit of the Council. And as a proverb says: "If a tree falls, it makes a great crash, but if a forest grows, nothing can be heard for a silent process is happening." Thus, in the din of an anti-Council sentiment and erroneous progressivism, the journey of the Church silently gathered momentum, with great suffering and great losses, as she built up a new cultural process.

Then came the second phase in 1989 — the collapse of the Communist regimes; but the response was not a return to the faith as one might have expected. It was not the rediscovery that the Church herself, with the authentic Council, had come up with the answer. The response instead was the total skepticism of so-called "post-modernity." It held that nothing is true, that everyone must live as best he can. Materialism gained ground, a pseudo-rationalist, blind skepticism that led to drugs and ended in all the problems we know. Once again, it closed the ways to faith because it was something so simple and so obvious. No, there was nothing true about it. The truth is intolerant, we cannot take this route.

Here, in the contexts of these two cultural ruptures: The first, the cultural revolution of 1968 and the second, the collapse, we might call it, into nihilism after 1989, the Church humbly set out among the afflictions of the world and the glory of the Lord. On this path we must grow, patiently, and must now learn in a new way what it means to give up triumphalism. The Council had said that triumphalism should be given up — and was thinking of the baroque, of all these great cultures of the Church. People said: Let us begin in a new and modern way. But another triumphalism had developed, that of thought: We now do things, we have found our way, and on this path we will find the new world. Yet, the humility of the Cross, of the Crucified One, excludes this same triumphalism.

We must renounce the triumphalism that holds that the great Church of the future is now truly being born.

Christ's Church is always humble and in this very way is great and joyful. It seems to me very important that our eyes are now open and can see all that is positive that developed in the period subsequent to the Council: in the renewal of the liturgy, in the Synods, the Roman Synods, the universal Synods, the diocesan synods, the parish structures, in collaboration, in the new responsibility of lay people, in the great intercultural and intercontinental co-responsibility, in a new experience of the Church's catholicity, of the unanimity that grows in humility and yet is the true hope of the world.

Thus, I think we have to rediscover the Council's great legacy. It is not a spirit reconstructed from texts but consists of the great Council texts themselves, reinterpreted today with the experiences we have had that have borne fruit in so many movements and so many new religious communities. I went to Brazil knowing that the sects were spreading and that the Catholic Church there seemed somewhat fossilized; but once I arrived there, I saw that a new religious community is born in Brazil almost every day, a new movement is born. Not only are the sects growing, the Church is growing with new situations full of vitality, not in order to complete the statistics — this is a false hope, statistics are not our god — but these situations are growing in souls and create the joy of faith, the presence of the Gospel; consequently, they are also creating a true development of the world and of society.

It seems to me, therefore, that we must combine the great humility of the Crucified One, of a Church that is always humble and always opposed by the great economic and military powers, etc., but with this humility we must also learn the true triumphalism of catholicity that develops in all the centuries.

Today, too, the presence of the Crucified and Risen One, who has preserved his wounds, is increasing. He is wounded, but it is in this way that he renews the world and gives his breath that also renews the Church, despite all our poverty. And I would say that it is in this combination of the humility of the Cross and the joy of the Risen Lord, who in the Council gave us a great signpost for our journey, that we can go ahead joyously and full of hope.

VII. Questions Asked by the Youth of Italy

The following questions were asked by Italian Youth during an encounter with Pope Benedict XVI on the Plain of Montorso in Loretto on September 1, 2007.

52.[61] *"Many of us young people in the suburbs do not have a center, a place or people with whom we can identify. Often we are without a history, a perspective or even a future. It seems that what we really wait for never happens. From this come the experience of solitude and, at times, an improper dependence on others. Your Holiness, is there someone or something by means of which we can become important? How is it possible to hope when reality negates every dream of happiness, every project of life?"*

THANK YOU FOR THIS QUESTION and for your very realistic presentation of the situation. It is not always easy to respond concerning the peripheries of this world with great problems and we do not want to live an easy optimism; but on the other hand, we must have the courage to go forwards.

I will therefore anticipate the essence of my answer: Yes, there is hope today too; each one of you is important because each is known and desired by God, and God has his plan for each one. It is our task to discover and respond to it, so that despite these precarious and marginalized situations, we will be able to put into practice God's plan for us.

However, to go into detail, you have realistically presented to us the situation of a society: In the outskirts it seems hard to move ahead, to change the world for the better. Everything seems concentrated in the great centers of economic and political power, the great bureaucracies dominate, and those in the outskirts truly seem excluded from this life.

---

[61] Question asked by Piero Tisti and Giovanna Di Mucci.

Then, one aspect of this situation of marginalization that affects so many people is that the important cells of social life that can also build centers on the fringes are fragmented: The family, which should be the place where generations meet — from great-grandfather to grandchild — should not only be a place where generations meet but also where they learn to live, learn the essential virtues, and this is in danger.

Thus, all the more should we do our utmost to ensure that the family survives, that today too, it is the vital cell, the center in the periphery.

Therefore, the parish, the living cell of the Church, must also really be a place of inspiration, life, and solidarity that helps people build together centers in the periphery. And I must say here, there is often talk about the Church in the suburbs and in the center, which would be Rome, but in fact in the Church there are no suburbs because where Christ is, the whole center is there.

Wherever the Eucharist is celebrated, wherever the tabernacle stands, there is Christ; hence, there is the center, and we must do all we can to ensure that these living centers are effective, present, and truly a force that counters this marginalization.

The living Church, the Church of the little communities, the parish Church, the movements, must form as many centers in the outskirts and thus help to overcome the difficulties that the leading politics obviously cannot manage to resolve, and, at the same time, we must also think that despite the great focuses of power, contemporary society itself is in need of solidarity, of a sense of lawfulness, of the initiative and creativity of all.

I know that this is easier said than done, but I see here people who are working to increase the number of centers in the peripheries, to increase hope, and thus it seems to me that we should take up the initiative. The Church must be present precisely in the suburbs; Christ must be present, the center of the world must be present.

We have seen and we see today in the Gospel that for God there are no peripheries. In the vast context of the Roman Empire, the Holy Land was situated on the fringe; Nazareth was on the margins, an unknown town. Yet that very situation was, de facto, to become the center that changed the world!

And thus, we must form centers of faith, hope, love, and solidarity, centers of a sense of justice and lawfulness and of cooperation. Only in this way will modern society be able to survive. It needs this courage, it needs to create centers even if, obviously, hope does not seem to exist. We must counter this desperation, we must collaborate with great solidarity in doing our best to increase hope, so that men and women may collaborate and live.

The world — we see it — must be changed, but it is precisely the mission of young people to change it! We cannot change it with our own strength alone but in communion of faith and in journeying on together. In communion with Mary, with all the saints, in communion with Christ, we can do something essential, and I encourage you and invite you to trust in Christ, to trust in God.

Being in the great company of the saints and moving forward with them can change the world, creating centers in the outskirts, so that the company of saints may truly become visible and thus the hope of all may become realistic, and every one may say: "I am important in the totality of history. The Lord will help us." Thank you.

⌐⌐⌐

53.[62] *"I believe in the God who has touched my heart, but I have many insecurities, questions, and fears that I carry within. It is not easy to speak about God with my friends; many of them see the Church as a reality that judges youth, that opposes their desire for happiness and love. Faced with this refusal, I feel all of my solitude as human and I want to feel near God. Your Holiness, in this silence, where is God?"*

YES, EVEN THOUGH WE ARE believers, we all know God's silence. In the Psalm we have just recited, there is this almost despairing cry: "Make haste to answer me, O Lord... Do not hide your face!" and a little while ago a book of the spiritual experiences of Mother Teresa was published, and what we already all knew was a little more clearly shown: With all her charity and the power of her faith, Mother Teresa suffered from God's silence.

On the one hand, we must also bear God's silence in order to understand our brothers who do not know God.

On the other, with the Psalm we can always cry to God once again: "Answer us, show your face!" And without a doubt, in our life, if our hearts are open, we can find the important moments when God's presence really becomes tangible even for us.

I now remember a little story that John Paul II told at the Spiritual Exercises he preached in the Vatican when he was not yet pope. He recounted that after the war he was visited by a

[62] Question asked by Sara Simonetta.

Russian official who was a scientist and who said to him as a scientist: "I am certain that God does not exist. Yet, if I am in the mountains, surrounded by his majestic beauty, by his grandeur, I am equally sure that the Creator does exist and that God exists."

The beauty of creation is one of the sources where we can truly touch God's beauty, we can see that the Creator exists and is good, which is true as Sacred Scripture says in the creation narrative — that is, that God conceived of this world and made it with his heart, his will, and his reason, and he found it good.

We too must be good in order to have an open heart and to perceive God's true presence. Then, hearing the Word of God in the solemn liturgical celebrations, in celebrations of faith, in the great music of faith, we feel this presence. I remember at this moment another little story that a bishop on his *ad limina* visit told me a little while ago.

There was a very intelligent woman who was not a Christian. She began to listen to the great music of Bach, Handel, and Mozart. She was fascinated and said one day: "I must find the source of this beauty" and the woman converted to Christianity, to the Catholic faith, because she had discovered that this beauty has a source, and the source is the presence of Christ in hearts — it is the revelation of Christ in this world.

Hence, great feasts of faith, of liturgical celebration, but also personal dialogue with Christ: He does not always respond, but there are times when he really responds. Then there is the friendship, the company of faith.

Now, gathered here in Loreto, we see that faith unites, friendship creates a company of traveling companions. And we sense that all this does not derive from nothing but truly has a source, that the silent God is also a God who speaks, that he reveals himself and, above all, that we ourselves can be witnesses of his presence, and from our faith a light truly shines also for others.

Thus, I would say on the one hand, we must accept that God is silent in this world, but we must not be deaf to his words or blind to his appearance on so many occasions. We see the Lord's presence, especially in creation, in the beautiful liturgy, in friendship within the Church, and full of his presence, we can also give light to others.

Thus, I come to the second part, or rather, the first part of your question: It is difficult to speak to friends today about God, and perhaps even more difficult to talk about the Church, because they see in God only the limit of our freedom, a God of commandments, of prohibitions, and the Church as an institution that limits our freedom, that imposes prohibitions upon us.

Nonetheless, we must try to make the living Church visible to them, not this idea of a center of power in the Church with these labels, but the community of companions where, in spite of all life's problems that exist for everyone, is born our joy of living.

Here, a third memory springs to mind. I was in Brazil, in Fazenda da Esperança, this great community where drug addicts are treated and rediscover hope, the joy of living in this world; and they witnessed what the actual discovery that God exists meant for their recovery from despair. They thus understood that their life has meaning, and they rediscovered the joy of being in this world, the joy of facing the problems of human life.

In every human heart, despite all the problems that exist, is a thirst for God, and when God disappears, the sun that gives light and joy also disappears.

This thirst for the infinite that is in our hearts is also demonstrated even in the reality of drugs: The human being wants to extend the quality of life, to have more than life, to have the infinite, but drugs are a lie, they are a fraud, because they do not extend life but destroy it.

The great thirst that speaks to us of God and sets us on the path that leads to him is true, but we must help one another. Christ came to create a network of communion in the world, where all together we might carry one another and thus help one another together to find the ways that lead to life and to understand that the commandments of God are not limits to our freedom but the paths that guide us to the other, towards the fullness of life.

Let us pray to the Lord to help us understand his presence, to be full of his revelation, his joy, to help one another to go forward in the company of faith and with Christ to increasingly find the true Face of God, and hence, true life.

Appendix I

Scripture References

Appendix II

Topical Index